Finding Quality Early Childcare

Finding Quality Early Childcare

A Step-by-Step Guide for Parents about What Matters Most

Sarah Taylor Vanover

ROWMAN & LITTLEFIELD
Lanham • Boulder • New York • London

Published by Rowman & Littlefield
A wholly owned subsidiary of The Rowman & Littlefield Publishing Group, Inc.
4501 Forbes Boulevard, Suite 200, Lanham, Maryland 20706
www.rowman.com

Unit A, Whitacre Mews, 26-34 Stannary Street, London SE11 4AB

British Library Cataloguing in Publication Information Available

Library of Congress Cataloging-in-Publication Data Available

ISBN 978-1-4758-2773-6 (cloth : alk. paper)
ISBN: 978-1-4758-2775-0 (electronic)

∞ ™ The paper used in this publication meets the minimum requirements of American National Standard for Information Sciences Permanence of Paper for Printed Library Materials, ANSI/NISO Z39.48-1992.

Printed in the United States of America

I dedicate this book to my family, who have been my constant cheerleaders!

Contents

Preface

Where do I go to find childcare for my baby? Where are the best preschools, and how do I get my child a spot in one of them? As soon as families begin thinking about childcare and preschool, I start to receive phone calls and e-mails. Friends or acquaintances to whom I have not spoken for years will track me down to start asking questions about which program is best for their baby.

Finding childcare can be tricky, because unless you know an expert in the field, you may not know where to start the search process. Some families will go strictly on the opinion of a friend; however, that friend may not be looking for the same standards in childcare. Some families will select a program close to their home or neighborhood for convenience, but does that program have an accreditation or another accountability system in place? Some families may wait until a couple of weeks before they need to start childcare, but for many programs, there may be an extensive waiting list already established.

All of these factors make it challenging for families to select high-quality childcare. Families want the safest, healthiest, and most educational program with the best teachers; however, many parents report that they do not know how to determine which early childhood education programs meet those standards. This text will look at all of the aspects of quality childcare to educate parents on their importance and help each family with the childcare selection process.

WHY IS IT IMPORTANT TO FIND QUALITY CHILDCARE?

Finding high-quality childcare for your young child is essential. The alternative can involve several different possibilities:

A lack of childcare:

When families wait too long to find a quality childcare environment, they often end up without any type of care. This can mean that one parent or family member may need to give up essential income from a job in order to stay home with the child. Some employers may be generous to offer a temporary leave, but eventually, every business must fill the position.

A poor-quality childcare environment:

When you are unable to find a spot for your child in the childcare program of your choice, you begin to look at less suitable options. Of course, childcare programs are not merely lumped into two categories: poor quality and high quality. Every program has strengths and weaknesses, but there are many programs that have more flaws than assets.

In order to feel comfortable leaving your child in someone else's care, it is essential to know that the child is safe, healthy, and left with adults who care for your child. When a family knows that a child is not in an environment with these minimum standards of care, then the family members either spend a great deal of time worrying about the child when they are apart, or the family pulls the child out of childcare and must start the entire process over again.

WHAT ARE THE BENEFITS OF SELECTING HIGH-QUALITY CHILDCARE?

Simply looking from the perspective of the adult, there are many personal benefits to selecting quality childcare!

- Knowing that your child is being cared for properly gives all families peace of mind. If your child is happy and safe, you can carry on with your normal daily activities without worrying about each moment of the child's day.
- If your child is in a high-quality childcare program, then you are more likely to attend work regularly. Programs that have high rates of illness and injury can keep a family going back and forth to the doctor's office. Also, if the family is worried about the child getting hurt each day, then they may keep the child home as a preventative measure. Frequent absences for the child mean frequent absences for the grown-ups.
- If your job is flexible and your employer does not mind these absences, then you are lucky to have such a family-friendly position. (Please keep in mind that even in quality childcare

programs, your child might get sick. When young children are learning to blow their noses, wash their hands, and use the toilet, the spread of germs is higher than any other age group; however, a quality program puts measures into place to eliminate as much illness as possible.)

- A quality childcare program not only provides care, but it also provides education for your child. If you want a babysitter to care for your child's basic needs (eating, diapering, sleeping, etc.), that is very different from an early childhood education program.

- A quality program will start the education process in the infant room by talking to your baby and letting the child have a variety of sensory experiences. In preschool, the children should be working on social skills, like playing together in a group and sharing, but the children should also be learning academic skills like counting, letter recognition, and basic handwriting development.

- A quality childcare program understands that a huge portion of school readiness includes the social and emotional development of the child. In order to succeed in Kindergarten, preschool teachers need to stress the importance of following a daily schedule, following two- and three-step instructions, playing in small groups and large groups, and sharing with peers. These skills are just as essential as academic skills, and should be represented equally in the curriculum.

- A high-quality childcare program will involve families in the education process. There should be many different ways that families are included in their children's education, for example, classroom newsletters, parent-teacher conferences, parent volunteers, and family activities like music performances or family dinners. The childcare program needs to make it evident that families are invited to participate at any time and that their involvement in their children's education is important to the education process.

- A quality early childhood program will also provide opportunities for parent education. Since the early childhood education specialists are experts on child development and children's behavior during this stage of life, it is important for the teachers and the program director to provide learning opportunities for the parents. This could be through a weekly blog that parents have the opportunity to read online, or the program might provide an education meeting once a semester to focus on a specific topic.

- High-quality early childhood programs have specific rules that both staff and enrolled families are expected to follow. These can be rules about discipline strategies, professional behavior on the campus, or about business principles like when to pay tuition. Programs that have these policies in place and have the policies readily available to staff and families are much more successful at handling difficult situations and giving fair and just treatment to each individual family.
- High-quality childcare programs have a high level of accountability. Although having the individualized care of a nanny or au pair in your home may seem tempting due to the flexible schedule and individualized care, this type of care has little accountability in place for the caregiver. In childcare programs, the providers are rarely left alone with children. Multiple caregivers take care of the children and see the children at all times.
- This means that instances of child abuse are extremely low in childcare program settings, and you get the benefit of your child learning to relate to more than one person's caregiving style. If a caregiver were to become frustrated with a child, then he or she can always ask for help from another provider in order to step away and calm down. Additionally, in a childcare program, the director is also supervising the childcare providers, which provides another level of accountability.
- Another benefit of a high-quality childcare setting is that childcare providers are specialized in child development and can recognize when a child may not be meeting developmental milestones on time. When these slight delays are identified at an early age, then the child is typically able to get assistance from a doctor or therapist and make great developmental strides before starting elementary school. It is harder to resolve the delay the longer the issue goes untreated.
- Finally, high-quality early childhood programs do an excellent job of providing a structured setting for children. It may be hard to believe, but young children truly crave structure. When children anticipate their daily schedule and know what to expect, then they are more likely to have more successful mealtimes, bedtimes, and transitions from one activity to another. A childcare program with an established daily routine

allows a child more comfort than changing plans each day based on particular activities.

WHAT DO I NEED TO KNOW ABOUT CHILDCARE?

This book will take a deeper look at individual areas of quality childcare that you need to consider when selecting care for your child. No program may have *every* characteristic in this book; however, it is important to look at a variety of characteristics and determine which you believe are the most important.

It is also important to determine the logistical characteristics that will be involved in your selection process. How much money can you spend on childcare? If the program is too expensive, are there scholarships available or does the program accept a subsidy program? What are the hours during which you will definitely need childcare? Is the program close enough to your home that you can drop your child off at school and still get to work on time?

These factors may need to be determined before you ever begin to tour programs and ask about the enrollment process so that you do not waste valuable time. In this book, we will also look at the following considerations:

- licenses, accreditations, and policies;
- models of learning;
- classroom placement;
- health and safety standards;
- teacher qualifications;
- curriculum and the classroom environment;
- childcare for children with special needs;
- infant childcare; and
- the transition to Kindergarten.

At the end of this book, there is a list of questions for evaluating childcare programs once you begin the process of touring centers. In order to see what is actually going on in the center and how the teachers relate to the children, it is essential to tour the facility before making any final decisions on where to place your child.

ONE

License, Accreditation, and Policies

Many families are confused as to the difference between a licensed childcare program and a program with an early childhood accreditation. If a program is licensed, then it must be a quality program, right? What must a childcare program have in order to be licensed? What makes an accredited program different from a licensed program? Is an accredited program better? These are all questions that families may face during the childcare selection process.

WHAT IS LICENSED CHILDCARE?

A state issues a license to a childcare program if it meets the minimum requirements for health, safety, supervision, and curriculum standards. These minimum standards are determined by each individual state, so a licensed childcare program in one state may not be able to meet the minimum requirements in another state. The license means that the program has permission to be open, but it does not mean that it is a quality establishment.

This process is similar to that which restaurants or hair salons must undergo in many states. In order to open for business to the public, the establishment must meet the minimum requirements, but there can be a great deal of difference in the quality of two licensed establishments. There is usually a separate licensing process for home-based childcare and childcare programs in a center (separate from a home).

1

WHAT DOES A LICENSE REQUIRE?

Although the requirements for a childcare license vary from state to state, most states look at the following areas to determine if a center should receive a license:

- student-to-teacher ratio: How many children can each adult watch safely? This number should be smaller for young children and increase as the children become more independent.
- maximum number of children: Each age group should have a maximum number of children allowed to be in the room in order to prevent too much chaos and allow proper supervision of the children.
- teacher education requirements and annual training
- health and safety procedures: This includes procedures for hand washing, diapering, cleaning and sanitizing the classrooms, immunization requirements for the children and staff members, administering medication to children, CPR and first aid training, and fire/safety drills.
- required staff paperwork, including background checks
- required student paperwork, including emergency contact information
- food preparation procedures: This can mean procedures for preparing meals at the facility or serving meals to the children that parents prepared at home. It also includes the procedures for preparing bottles and formula for infants.
- facility requirements: This includes inspections by the fire marshal and the health department to look at emergency exits and the kitchen structure. This part of the license also inspects the building materials, plumbing and air-conditioning, and the zoning permit for the building.
- number of children allowed in the building based on the square footage
- lesson plan and curriculum requirements

When a childcare program receives a license from the state, then the licensing body typically does an inspection before the program opens and will conduct announced and unannounced visits throughout the year. If a program meets all of its licensing requirements each year (with minimal violations), then the licensing organization may only conduct an annual visit; however, if a family or a community member lodges a complaint against the center, then there will be unannounced visits that follow.

WHAT IS ACCREDITATION?

Accreditation is a quality assurance process for early childhood education programs. The accreditation organization is usually separate from the organization that offers a license. It may be a nonprofit organization like NAEYC, the National Association for the Education of Young Children, which offers the accreditation; however, many states have now set up their own quality rating system for early childhood programs. Although the state-run program is still administered by a government office, it is typically through a department separate from licensure.

When a childcare program receives an accreditation, that accreditation is like a contract to the families that the program will maintain higher quality standards. If the childcare program does not maintain those standards, then the organization can take away the accreditation.

HOW DOES A CHILDCARE PROGRAM BECOME ACCREDITED?

The accreditation process can be very lengthy and expensive for many early education programs. The accrediting body usually requires an application and proof of education of the staff members employed at the center. Many accrediting organizations will require the program, and sometimes the classroom teachers, to put together a portfolio outlining how the center meets the accreditation standards that are required.

Almost all accreditation reviews end with an onsite observation of the facility and the classrooms. The accrediting organization typically uses a standardized assessment tool to grade the program on meeting the standards.

There can also be large fees involved when applying for an accreditation, and the fees are required in advance, regardless of whether the program meets its goals. Some of the accreditations run by state funding have found ways to give programs financial incentives for reaching higher tiers of accreditation. Many of these state programs can require a national accreditation to accompany the state accreditation.

Regardless of which accreditation a childcare program pursues, the process is usually very lengthy and requires a lot of additional work on the part of the teachers and the administrators. Childcare programs willingly participate in this process in order to show families the high levels of care that they offer young children.

WHO ARE THE ACCREDITING ORGANIZATIONS?

There are several different organizations that offer quality childcare accreditation:

- The National Association for the Education of Young Children (NAEYC) is a national early childhood education professional development organization that promotes quality education and care for children from birth through age eight. NAEYC has a four-step accreditation process that holds early education programs accountable to its ten program standards: relationships, curriculum, teaching, assessment of child progress, health, teachers, families, community relationships, physical environment, and management and leadership.
- The National Early Childhood Program Accreditation (NECPA) was founded in 1991 with the sole purpose of encouraging higher quality early childhood education programs through a reputable and affordable accreditation process. NECPA established its accreditation process on its core values of integrity, pursuit of excellence, responsibility, reliability, and commitment. NECPA uses a research-based approach to accreditation.
- The National Accreditation Commission for Early Care and Education Programs (NACECE) is a national accreditation organization that has over fifteen hundred accredited centers in over thirty-eight states. NACECE works with a wide variety of early childhood programs including Head Start, public school preschool, college-campus childcare programs, private childcare programs, faith-based preschools, corporate childcare centers, employer-sponsored programs, and Montessori programs.
- Association Montessori Internationale (AMI) is an international professional development organization for Montessori teachers that also offers a structured accreditation process for Montessori schools. AMI certification primarily focuses on training teachers on the teachings of Dr. Maria Montessori, but schools can receive approval and certification as an AMI school. This means that the school is held accountable to the highest standards of the AMI.

- The American Montessori Society (AMS) is a professional development organization for Montessori teachers that was established in 1960 by Dr. Nancy McCormick Rambusch, when interest in Montessori education in the United States began to grow. AMS also provides a school accreditation system, and currently over twelve hundred schools are AMS accredited. These schools must meet the AMS school accreditation standards and criteria and adhere to the AMS code of ethics.
- HighScope Educational Research Foundation is a nonprofit organization based in Ypsilanti, Michigan, which endorses active participation learning. The foundation offers teacher training programs and certifications, but it also offers an accreditation process for schools that adhere to the highest standards of the HighScope teaching standards.
- As the United States has realized the importance of early childhood education, many states have implemented their own quality rating system for childcare programs in order to encourage all early education programs to be accountable to quality learning standards.

Based on your state, the accreditation program is probably based in the Division of Childcare or the Department of Education. Most of the state government accreditation programs have multiple tiers or percentage ratings like a hotel or a restaurant in order to let the public evaluate which programs are of the highest quality and which programs still have room for growth.

If a preschool program is a part of an elementary school, then it may share the accreditation with the school as a whole. The accrediting organizations that supervise primary and secondary education are very different than those that only work with early childhood education; however, the main purpose of the organization is to still hold the school accountable to the highest education standards.

If the childcare program possesses an accreditation that you have never heard of, it is important to do your research and find out about the standards that the school is responsible for maintaining.

CENTER POLICIES

Along with licensing and accreditation standards, it is also very important for an early childhood program to have its own set of policies and procedures. Every center should have a family handbook that shares the policies that pertain to enrolled families.

It is also important for each childcare program to have a staff handbook with the policies that relate specifically to being an employee in the program. Staff members must be familiar with both staff policies and family policies in order to perform their jobs effectively.

The family handbook does not need to be extensive, but it does need to address topics about which families may have frequent questions. It also needs to address school procedures. A typical family handbook will cover topics like

- the enrollment process
- tuition costs and additional fees
- payment methods
- policy on withdrawal
- required forms
- procedures on administering medication
- daily schedule for the children
- description of the center curriculum
- school policy on behavior management and redirection
- items the family is expected to bring to school
- clothing that children should wear to school
- illness policy
- biting policy
- safety procedures and drills
- child abuse and neglect procedures
- parent participation and conferences
- parent behavior on school property
- grievance procedures
- causes (if any) for dismissal from the program

When the program has these types of procedures established and provides them to the families upon enrollment, then the families and the program administrators know what to anticipate from one another. If the school policies are more vague, then it can be difficult for the administration to negotiate a tricky situation. Program management is a key factor of quality early education, so it is essential for programs to be prepared to handle difficult situations.

- Does the program meet the minimum licensing standards to be open? Is there a report from the last licensing visit (at the center or online through the licensing body) that you can view?

- Does the program have an accreditation beyond the minimum operation standards?
- Is there a parent handbook with the center policies available to each family enrolled?

TWO

Models of Learning

There are so many different styles of preschools and childcare programs to consider when you are selecting a program for your child. Each style has positive attributes, but it is important to understand the differences among the programs so that you can choose the one that best suits your child and your family. Some programs have different educational philosophies, and some have eligibility criteria like income level.

Depending on the area in which you live, you may not have access to all of these types of childcare programs. Also, some childcare programs may be full-day programs that appeal to working families, but other programs may be half-day or require families to volunteer in the classroom a certain amount during the course of each month. When you consider each program, it is important to keep these different characteristics in mind.

TEACHER CENTERED VS. CHILD CENTERED

There are two different philosophies on child independence in the classroom: teacher centered and child centered. Most classrooms incorporate some of each of these, but you can observe the classroom to get a sense of which philosophy the classroom primarily follows.

Teacher Centered

In a teacher-centered classroom, the teacher is the primary source of learning. There are teacher-directed activities where the teacher is offering knowledge to the students. The teacher selects which activities the children may do, and the teacher sets a strict daily schedule that everyone in the classroom must follow.

In this style of classroom, the main learning activity of the day is a large-group activity where the teacher leads songs, reads a story, and teaches the children a lesson on the day's subject.

Child Centered

A child-centered classroom follows the interests and needs of the child over those of the teacher. The teacher plans activities for the children, but the classroom is based on the children exploring the materials and playing independently and in small groups. The teacher creates a classroom schedule but allows some flexibility if the children are very engaged in a learning activity. The teacher plans materials and activities that are interesting to the children instead of planning the same lessons from a previous year.

Most early childhood education specialists believe that a predominantly child-centered curriculum is best for the children; however, there may still be some teacher-directed activities in this setting.

STYLES OF LEARNING

Play-Based Philosophy

The play-based early childhood philosophy is often called the developmentally appropriate classroom. This means that the classroom environment and the teacher meet children at their current level of development and encourage them to meet achievable goals. The classroom must be appropriate both for the age of the children and the development level of the children.

The classroom philosophy is based on the most current research of how children learn, and teachers must acquire ongoing professional training to meet the needs of their students in the best way possible. This learning environment addresses all the domains of child development, including physical development (health, fine motor, and gross motor), social and emotional development, language development, self-help skills, and cognitive development.

The play-based classroom is the most common style of early childhood education in the United States. It is a child-centered model of learning that believes that children learn best through play and when they choose activities based on their own interests. These classrooms are built on a foundation of creativity, confidence, and motivation.

Each child has the opportunity to develop at his or her own pace, and the teacher encourages that development process. Teachers are responsible for setting up the learning environment and providing materials that interest and motivate the children to explore.

The curriculum in a developmentally appropriate classroom is important, but its importance is outweighed by the teaching practices of the instructor. The teachers must engage the children in order to avoid conflict in the classroom. Also, the teachers play with the children and engage them with open-ended questions to further their learning and encourage problem solving.

The classroom provides open-ended materials like art, blocks, pretend play materials, and sand and water play. The classroom setting also encourages cooperation with materials for group play like blocks, musical instruments, pretend play toys, and daily circle time.

Developmentally appropriate classrooms place a strong emphasis on teaching children social and emotional skills and self-help skills. Social and emotional skills in the early childhood classroom include getting along with others, sharing, resolving conflict, and expressing emotions. Self-help skills for young children include making decisions, dressing skills, toileting, and feeding skills.

The entire classroom group comes together each day for circle time, meals and snacks, and for nap time, but the children will never sit down for extended periods of time. The length of any activity is based on the development level of the child and his or her ability to concentrate on the same task.

Although play-based classrooms are the predominant learning environment in the United States, many play-based programs will blend their classroom setting with another educational philosophy. For example, you may see a play-based classroom that has some characteristics of a Montessori classroom or a Reggio Emilia school, but they will not adopt the entire philosophy of the program.

Montessori Education

The Italian physician Maria Montessori created the Montessori education system. She spent a great deal of time observing how young children learn and interact with others, and then she developed the Montessori learning approach and created hands-on learning materials that allow students to explore the classroom with their senses.

She first developed her education theory while working with children who lived on the streets in Italy and came from poverty or had some type of developmental delay. Montessori classrooms are child centered. Maria Montessori believed that play was the work of the child. Each child has a motivation and need to work and discover each day.

Montessori classrooms are set up for children to select their work and repeat that activity again and again until they have mastered the skill. Montessori preschool classrooms provide curriculum in practical life, sensory skills, language and reading, math, science, geography, and the arts. Montessori toddler programs focus on some of the same skill areas, but they focus more on basic care needs, independence, practical life skills, and sensory skills.

Montessori classrooms are multiage classrooms that allow for a child to spend three years in the same classroom environment. For example, preschool students stay in the same Montessori classroom while they are three, four, and five years old.

This multiage experience is based on the "See It, Do It, Teach It" philosophy. Young students in the classroom learn by watching their more experienced peers, and the oldest students in the classroom are able to solidify their own learning by teaching the newest students how to use the materials.

The Montessori classroom allows children to move freely throughout the classroom to select their own choices, but it also teaches children a great deal of responsibility to care for the materials properly and put them away when they are finished. The Montessori classroom is based on intrinsic motivation (the child's interest and motivation to learn) instead of rewards, grades, and incentives to encourage student participation.

Reggio Emilia Programs

The Reggio Emilia philosophy was created by Loris Malaguzzi. This movement is centered on the belief that young children develop their true personalities during early childhood and they use many different methods to express themselves. This is often referred to as the "hundred languages of young children."

This teaching philosophy is child centered and based on responsibility, respect, and community. This philosophy is also very exploratory and discovery based. It has a self-guided curriculum that allows children to interact with materials that they are most interested in using.

Unlike some philosophies, the teacher is viewed as a *co-learner* with the students in this setting. The teacher's task is to plan lessons and arrange the learning environment based on the interests of the children. Reggio Emilia programs do not use structured curriculums or standardized tests. The teachers use work samples (e.g., drawings, art, and journals) or quotes and pictures of the students to document their progress.

The Reggio Emilia classroom focuses on intrinsic motivation, so teachers do not use grades or rewards to encourage student achievements. The classroom environment, the students, and the teacher are all seen as equally important pieces of the learning experience. Similar to the Montessori classroom, the students stay with one particular teacher for a three-year cycle to establish consistency and attached relationships.

This type of classroom is often referred to as the Project Approach because the teachers will often select a long-term learning project for the classroom based on the interests of the students. For example, a Reggio Emilia classroom may spend an entire month studying sharks if the students continue to show interest in learning about this topic.

The teacher will learn with the students, and together they will use the theme of sharks to incorporate science, art, literacy, math, and vocabulary skills into the classroom. Teachers begin a project by observing the students for a week or two and identifying their interests. Then the teacher will adapt the environment to provide materials that relate to the projects. These projects can last for a large part of the semester if students continue to show interest in learning.

HighScope Education

David Weikart was the primary developer of the HighScope education philosophy in Ypsilanti, Michigan, in the 1960s. This method is used in preschool and elementary school settings, and it is based on the developmental theories of Jean Piaget, John Dewey, and Lev Vygotsky.

Vygotsky believed in the learning process of scaffolding, which means that adults assist children at their current developmental level and then encourage them to meet the next developmental milestone with adult assistance. Once the child can achieve that goal independently, the adult can reduce the assistance provided.

HighScope encourages the adult to be a *facilitator* in the classroom instead of a direct instructor or a supervisor. Like the Montessori education movement, this philosophy was designed to help children who were at risk due to living in poverty.

One of the key concepts of the HighScope classroom is "Plan, Do, and Review." During the initial large-group session of the day, the teacher will ask each student what he or she plans to do during the class free time. After free time, when the class meets together again, the teacher will ask each of the students to review the activities they completed during free time and if those were the activities that the children had planned on doing during the day.

The HighScope educational program is also based on active learning, a high-quality learning environment, a predictable daily routine, adult-child interactions, assessment, and conflict resolution. Children in the HighScope classroom will learn approaches to learning, language and literacy, social and emotional development, physical development and health, mathematics, science and technology, social studies, and the creative arts.

Waldorf Education

The Waldorf education philosophy was created by the Austrian educator and philosopher Rudolf Steiner. It follows a humanistic approach to education with a foundation on the value of human beings, individualism, an emphasis on developing community, and critical thinking. This is a child-centered approach, but there is a definite component that focuses on the group dynamic.

The Waldorf philosophy divides development of children and adolescents into three categories: early childhood for children from birth to age six, elementary education for children from seven years to age fourteen, and secondary education for children ages fourteen and older.

The early childhood stage of development focuses on hands-on activities and creative play. During the early years, there is a large focus on the arts and creative expression instead of on academic skills. There is also a large focus on being a member of the community.

The overarching goals for Waldorf education include independence, moral responsibility, being a member of a group, and social competence. This is another education philosophy where the teacher is a co-learner with the students.

Teachers and students have a great deal of autonomy in the classroom, and the teacher follows the interests and needs of the students to create curriculum and the learning environment. Teachers track student progress by using observation, student work samples, and conversations with the children. Waldorf schools use some standardized testing, but it is typically reserved to help the students prepare for college and is not used as frequently as it is in traditional public schools.

Waldorf classrooms place a lot of emphasis on the natural environment. Teachers encourage the use of natural materials (instead of plastic toys). They also utilize the outdoor classroom as much as possible. The goal of the Waldorf classroom is to establish a love of learning with intrinsic motivation to learn new concepts.

Steiner, the creator of the Waldorf movement, wanted to establish a spiritual but nondenominational setting for the children and the teachers, thus the emphasis on nature, respect for others, and the value of all human beings.

Waldorf programs typically keep students together in cohorts as they move through their education in order to establish a family-like social group for the students. Teachers usually stay with the same group of students for several years, depending on the individual school. "Lower school" teachers may stay with students for up to eight years as they complete their entire elementary education.

Head Start and Early Head Start

Head Start is a federally funded early childhood program that focuses on early childhood education, health, nutrition, and parent involvement. The program began in 1965 through Lyndon B. Johnson's "Great Society" campaign to assist children who were living in poverty. The goal was to help these children be more prepared to start Kindergarten and to provide services to children with and without special needs.

Head Start is for children three years of age until they are eligible to start Kindergarten. Early Head Start was added in 1994 and is for children from birth to age three. Early Head Start also offers prenatal programs.

The goals of Early Head Start are to focus on prenatal outcomes, healthy families, and infant and toddler development. Head Start goals include healthy development (across developmental areas) for children from three to five years of age.

Head Start also provides care for children of migrant or seasonal farm workers for children six months of age through five years of age. To qualify for Early Head Start or Head Start services, the family must earn less than 100 percent of the federal poverty level, although programs may make some exceptions for children who have special needs or families that require other services.

The Head Start framework focuses on five main domains of development for young children: language and literacy, cognition and general knowledge, approaches to learning, physical development and health, and social and emotional development.

Parent Cooperative Preschool Programs

Co-op preschool programs are groups of parents that come together to hire a primary teacher for the preschool classroom and take turns assisting the teacher in the classroom on a rotating basis. Families (or a board of elected families) share in the administrative duties of the preschool.

This type of program allows parents to observe how a professional teacher guides the students in the classroom and prepares lessons for them. Also, parents have the opportunity to learn about all the work that is involved in being a teacher. Many families in co-op preschools have the opportunity to learn about child development by observing their own children and other children the same age.

The educational philosophy of a co-op preschool will vary based on the individual program; however, the vast majority of these programs are play based. In order to participate in a co-op preschool, the family must have a least one adult who can participate in the classroom volunteering rotation.

Faith-Based Education

A faith-based preschool program serves families wanting their children to have an age-appropriate religious education that also includes an emphasis on the primary areas of child development. A faith-based program can follow any of the educational philosophies and add the component of religious education to the rest of the curriculum. Depending on the individual school, it will vary how much of the curriculum is dedicated to religious education.

Some faith-based education programs may only provide early childhood education to families that currently practice that faith, but others may open enrollment to all families that are interested in attending. For families that are interested in sending their children to faith-based education, it is essential for parents to contact the program for more information about the amount of religious education offered during the school day and to see if the doctrine of the school aligns with their personal beliefs.

Inclusive Childcare Programs

Inclusive early childhood classrooms focus on serving children with and without special needs in an inclusive environment. The educational philosophy of the program can vary, but the school must have a plan to focus on individualized education for the children in the classroom since the developmental ability levels of the children can vary greatly. Inclusive childcare programs should have teaching staff who have had specific training on how to work with children with disabilities.

There should also be a support system in place in the program where the early childhood center has therapists on staff (occupational therapists, speech and language pathologists, physical therapists, or behavior therapists) or they partner with the families' therapists to allow the therapists to come to the school to work with the children in the natural environment.

This type of learning setting often benefits both children with and without disabilities. Children without special needs often solidify their own learning by teaching their peers, and these students learn a great appreciation for diversity. Children with special needs have positive role models in the classroom and teachers who are trained to work with their conditions.

It is important for inclusive early childhood programs to have some type of system for selecting the ratio of children with special needs compared to children without special needs in the classroom in order to make sure that there are positive peer role models in every classroom setting and that the teacher is not overwhelmed by the amount of student needs.

DOING YOUR RESEARCH

Every early childhood program that you consider for your child will have positive and negative characteristics. You need to consider your family preferences and your child's individual needs. It is also important to do as much research as possible on the individual program that you are considering.

If the childcare program has a license, then you should be able to contact the state licensing body to view the past several reviews that the center has had or any filed reports that have been made against the center. Most states now have these reviews and complaints available online for prospective and current families to view as needed.

It is also important to contact the center to set up a tour of the facility and meet the teaching staff. Come prepared with a list of questions (see appendix 3) to ask during the tour. Also remember to ask the program to show you a copy of the parent handbook so that you can see the school policies.

The tour and the handbook will also help you determine if the program is right for your child. If the childcare program has any type of accreditation, look up the website for the accreditation and review the education philosophy and the accreditation requirements.

Finally, it is also important to listen to "word of mouth" reviews by families with children who are currently enrolled or who have graduated from the program. If the family felt safe leaving their child in the teachers' care and was happy with the school's parent-teacher communication and educational structure, then that speaks a great deal.

- Which model of learning does the program implement?
- Does the philosophy of this learning model seem to meet the needs of your child?

THREE

Classroom Placement

When a childcare program plans out the classroom placement list for the upcoming year, it can be a very difficult process. The administrative team must consider the teaching teams, the combinations of students in the classroom, the developmental needs of the children, the needs of each family as a whole, and a system for how children will be moved from classroom to classroom. Many families make requests for their children to have a specific teacher or a peer in the same classroom, but the childcare program has so many puzzle pieces to fit together that individual requests may not always be possible.

Larger programs may have more flexibility when selecting classroom placement because they may have more than one classroom with the same age groups of students. Small childcare programs may not have as many options for each age group. In order to be as efficient as possible, most childcare programs adhere to a philosophy of classroom placement that guides the program as they move children from one classroom to another. There are three predominant philosophies that childcare programs can select: moving children by age milestones, moving children after a yearlong placement, or using multiage classroom settings.

MOVING CHILDREN BY AGE MILESTONES

Some early childhood programs prefer to keep children together by the age range of the children. This allows teachers to specialize in working with a particular developmental range and give those children the most appropriate materials and environment for that age. This system allows the individual child to move to the next classroom when he or she is ready. For example, the center may have a classroom for nonmobile infants, mobile infants, young toddlers, older toddlers, two-year-olds, three-year-olds, and four-year-olds. A larger center may have the same age range classrooms but offer more than one room in each age range.

The environment is always prepared for the age of the children enrolled in the classroom, so the teachers do not have to transition materials in and out of the classroom as children meet new milestones. When an infant enrolls in this type of program, he or she may have multiple sets of teachers within the first year of care depending on when the child hits a new milestone or age range. Another consideration is that children move from classroom to classroom *individually* instead of transitioning with peers.

Once the child has been through this process several times, then he or she will probably know students in the next classroom that transitioned previously. This type of setting is used more frequently in year-round childcare programs so that the center can continue to accept new students whenever the families need to enroll. The administrative team may keep several openings in the older preschool classrooms to have the opportunity to transition younger students up to new classrooms and allow more infants admission to the program.

YEARLONG CLASSROOM PLACEMENT

A yearlong classroom placement in an early childhood classroom will look very similar to the structure of an elementary school. At the beginning of the school year, the children will be assigned to one classroom with a peer group and a teaching team that should remain together for a calendar year.

The children have the opportunity to develop stronger attachments with the teachers and with their peers since they are in the same classroom for a longer period of time. Teachers learn how to soothe and motivate their students, since they spend a greater amount of time learning about the children and the families. The children learn a consistent schedule for their classroom and a consistent set of rules.

Of course, due to the nature of early childhood education, the teaching staff could still change or peers may leave the program, but this yearlong placement does reduce some unneeded changes for the children. With this type of classroom placement, the ability levels of the children can change dramatically over the course of twelve months, particularly for the infant and toddler classrooms. If the children were all sleeping in cribs at the beginning of the school year, will they need to sleep on napping mats as they become more mobile? Does the childcare program have the resources to adapt the classroom and provide napping mats instead of cribs?

Also, the children in a toddler classroom may not be ready to begin toilet training during the first semester of the school year, but this may change in the spring semester. Does the classroom have access to child-sized toilets? Many childcare programs have limited resources, so it is important to ask the teachers how they will adapt the classroom for young children as the school year progresses and the children achieve more developmental milestones. This may not be a cause for concern in preschool classrooms since many of the toys and materials are the same for three-, four-, and five-year-old students.

MULTIAGE CLASSROOM PLACEMENT

There are several different philosophies of early childhood education that focus on using multiage classroom settings for the benefit of the children. Montessori classrooms, Reggio Emilia programs, Waldorf classrooms, and Head Start/Early Head Start programs all endorse a multiage classroom model. There are several benefits to having students of different ability levels grouped together in the same classroom setting. These philosophies are based on the "See It, Do It, Teach It" model that is used in many medical training programs throughout the world.

The youngest children in the classroom have the benefit of watching their peers use the materials in the classroom appropriately and follow the classroom rules. This teaches the youngest students how to use the classroom. As the children mature, they can complete the activities on their own and they require less assistance from teachers and peers. This establishes feelings of confidence and independence. Once a child is one of the oldest students in the classroom, then he or she can teach a young student how to complete a task.

Knowing the materials and rules well enough to teach someone else how to use them solidifies the child's own knowledge. This model is used in many three-year-old to five-year-old classrooms to complete the learning cycle. In infant and toddler classrooms, many programs will keep children together from birth until the age of three. These classrooms are much smaller than preschool classrooms because the classroom must follow a student-to-teacher ratio set by the youngest child in the room.

The benefit of this style of classroom for infants and toddlers is that it ensures that all the children get the individualized care and attention they need. When an infant room is full of nonmobile babies, there is a great demand on the teacher to assist the children and hold them at every moment. When there is a mixture of infants and toddlers, the varied levels of independence allow the teachers to meet the needs of each child more appropriately. Of course, in order to have a multiage infant and toddler classroom, then the program must have materials and resources for all the different ages of children in the room.

Both infant and toddler multiage classrooms and preschool multiage classrooms allow children to stay with their teachers and peer groups for longer amounts of time so that the children can establish attachment bonds with the adults and the other children in the room. A multiage classroom setting also allows children to be in a more diverse classroom and see children who are more advanced and children who are similar to one another.

Although a multiage classroom can have many benefits, it can be very challenging for teachers who have not been properly trained on this educational approach or for teachers who are lacking resources for their classrooms. When a preschool teacher is strained by the diverse range of children in the classroom, then he or she may focus on working with the oldest children in the classroom so that he or she can prepare these students for Kindergarten. The younger students may receive less time and attention from the teacher in this setting.

In the infant and toddler classroom you can see the reverse of this. The teachers may end up spending most of their time with the youngest infants because they have the most demanding basic needs routine. The most successful multiage classrooms have provided the teachers specific training on how to balance the needs of all the students in the classroom setting.

If you are considering a multiage classroom setting for your child, it is also important to ask the childcare program *how they divide students into the classroom.* Is there an equal division of children of different ages and abilities? This is very important in order to make a multiage classroom successful. If an infant and toddler classroom has many young infants with only one toddler, then the toddler is at a disadvantage since the classroom will be focused toward the young infants.

The same thing is true in the preschool classroom. If the classroom has many three-year-old students, then it may be challenging for the teacher to provide developmentally appropriate activities for only one or two older students. Make sure to ask the childcare program how they select students for a multiage classroom to meet the needs of all the students enrolled.

ADDITIONAL QUESTIONS

There are a few additional questions that you may want to ask a childcare program when considering how the administrative team places children into classrooms:

- Does the school typically keep twins together or do they have a policy to separate them into different classrooms? Do they ask the family for their preferences?
- This may also be a question to ask about siblings, if the children are in a multiage classroom setting. It is important that you feel comfortable with the program policy.
- Does the school allow teachers to have their own children in the classroom?
- Some teachers have mastered the skill of being a teacher and a parent at the same time, but many teachers can struggle if they have their son or daughter in their own classroom. Sometimes the teachers favor their own children above others, but in most cases, the teacher is harder on his or her own child. Inevitably, this situation takes time and attention away from the rest of the students in the classroom.
- Does the childcare program try to keep the same groups of peers together as they move through the center, or do they attempt to split students up from year to year in order to help students establish new relationships?
- It is important for families to know if the children will be together from year to year just so they know to anticipate changes in the future.

- How does the program attempt to handle a personality conflict between a teacher and a child or between a teacher and a family? Does the administrative team attempt to mediate between the family and the teaching staff, or are students moved to a new classroom at the request of the family?

Since teachers and peers share such a large portion of your child's day when he or she attends an early care and education program, it is very important to understand how the center places children into their classrooms for your own peace of mind. Make sure that you understand the process and how long your child is expected to stay in the same classroom with the same teachers and peers.

- Will your child be in a multiage classroom or in a classroom with children of the same age?
- Will your child be in the same classroom for a full school year, or will he or she be moved more frequently?
- Will your child move classrooms with the same peer group, or will he or she move to the next room on an individual schedule?

FOUR

Health and Safety Standards

A healthy and safe environment is typically the top priority of every family selecting a childcare program. Obviously, you will not leave your child in a childcare program that poses risks to your child! But not all safety hazards are obvious. At first glance, a program may not reveal potential problems, so it is important to ask questions.

There are also health and safety issues in group care that would not be an issue for you in your own home. As you select a group childcare program, it is important to make sure that all essential health and safety precautions are in place.

All childcare programs must obtain a license from the state in order to operate, and the vast majority of requirements for the license are health and safety standards. Each center is inspected annually to see if it continues to meet the licensing expectations. Families may review these licensing requirements. Depending on the state in which you live, the licensing regulations may be supervised by the Division of Childcare or by the Department of Education. In this chapter, we will look specifically at health and safety obligations, teacher requirements, and continuing education responsibilities.

When the licensing organization comes to review the childcare program, it will leave a report of how the program did in comparison to the licensing regulations. In many states, you can access these records in an online database. You can contact your state's Division of Childcare or Department of Education to find out how to access this type of database. The program may also be required to post this report in the center for families to review.

Almost all childcare programs have small violations during each visit. These can be as minimal as a top being left off of a bottle in the infant room, but more significant violations may include a child being unsupervised or a childcare provider falling asleep while caring for children. When you inspect a childcare program, you may want to review the comments from the program's last licensing inspection to see what type of violations the center experienced.

RATIOS

One of the first questions you should ask a potential childcare program is this: What student-to-teacher ratio is used in the classrooms? This refers to the maximum amount of children that may be left alone with a single adult at any given time. The adult can give higher quality care to the children when he or she is responsible for a smaller number of students. Lower student-to-teacher ratios allow for reduced injuries and more individualized learning in the classroom. In most childcare programs, the ratios for student-to-adult care will change based on the age of the children. For example, an infant room may have a 1:4 ratio, with one adult for every four children, but a preschool classroom may have a 1:10 ratio, with one adult for every ten preschool children.

The youngest children require the smallest child-to-adult ratios. This is because the adults must give so much additional time to each child for feeding, diapering, and putting each child to sleep. As children become older and more independent, the student-to-teacher ratio will increase slightly. The age of the youngest child in the classroom will always establish the ratio for the entire room.

The licensing body will establish a minimum ratio that must be kept in order for the program to maintain its license (e.g., one adult can care for up to five infants); however, high-quality childcare programs may lower that ratio to maintain a higher level of care. High-quality programs will further lower the child-to-adult ratio if there are children with special needs in the classroom who need more individual assistance. Special accreditations, like an accreditation from the National Association for the Education of Young Children, will require a lower ratio as well.

Along with ratios, you should also consider the total number of children that will be placed in the classroom. Even when a program has a reasonable ratio, the total number of children in the classroom at one time can still cause a safety issue. If a program has a 1:9 ratio for adults to students, that is a reasonable preschool ratio. However, the classroom will look *very* different if it has two adults with eighteen students compared to three adults with twenty-seven students. Many states establish a classroom maximum in their regulations in order to make sure that early childhood classrooms do not become too overwhelming for the adults and the children.

SUPERVISION

Supervision is a key component of a safe classroom for students of all ages. This simply refers to the teachers' awareness of what is going on in the classroom. This is a skill that develops over time for most teachers, but as a parent observer, there are several things that you can look for to see how the teacher is supervising the classroom. The media has revealed horror stories about children who had been left on school buses or on local playgrounds, and these obviously represent the worst-case scenario of poor supervision.

Keeping Track of Students

A teacher with true classroom awareness always knows how many students he or she is supervising at any given minute. These teachers may carry a clipboard around to document where each student is, have a dry-erase board posted in the room with the current head count, or they may simply know off the top of their heads the number of students in the room at each moment. Teachers will not have a student randomly wander off or get left behind if they are constantly counting every head in the classroom.

It is also essential that the teacher can *see* each child in the classroom at all times. Teachers who are aware of the children in the classroom will not stand with their backs to the majority of the students. You can see these teachers position themselves in such a manner that they can work individually with one child but still see every other student in the room. Skilled teachers very rarely sit in one position too long. In order to prevent potential problems from arising, they will circulate throughout the classroom to see how each group of students is interacting.

Circulation

In a classroom with a team of teachers, you will often see teachers taking turns to circulate. When one teacher is sitting down having an interaction with a small group of students, the other teacher will move throughout the room to assist other students. Then the team may switch roles as other students need more assistance.

Circulation is especially essential on the playground. You should be able to see teachers moving throughout the playground so that they can be close enough to intervene if a student could potentially get hurt. You should also be able to see this in the toddler classroom when children are learning to interact with others for the first time. If there is a child in the classroom who may bite or scratch another child when frustrated, then the teacher needs to remain close enough to intercede whenever it is possible.

Accidents and Abuse

Close supervision can significantly reduce the number of accidents and injuries in the classroom. Many childcare programs will include this high level of activity in a teacher's job description or require a doctor's physical examination to make sure that the teaching staff is able to get up and down from the floor constantly and move around the room easily. In order to supervise young children properly, teachers must have the physical energy to keep up with the pace of the classroom!

Supervision is also proactive. Teachers can properly supervise their classrooms by establishing positive safety rules in the classroom, like asking the children to use their walking feet and gentle hands (as opposed to saying "no hitting" and "no running"). Wise teachers know to give children positive directions and models of appropriate behavior instead of retroactively telling the children to stop a negative behavior.

When childcare providers closely supervise the children in their care, they learn many details about the children. They learn about a child's favorite stuffed animal or his favorite snack at snack time. They also learn when a child may be going through a traumatic situation outside of the center. In order to provide safe and healthy supervision, all childcare providers must know how to identify the signs of child abuse and know how to make a report if they suspect a child is being abused.

When touring a potential childcare facility, make sure to see if the program has a policy on mandatory reporting. All childcare providers are legally obligated to report suspicion of child abuse if they have seen signs of reasonable cause. This contact information should also be available to you and other families enrolled in the program in the event you have a concern about a child's well-being.

REDUCING INJURY

All young children have accidents. It is inevitable. As soon as your children learn to walk, they fall down. As soon as they learn to climb, they fall off of something. As soon as children are mobile—but not yet verbal—they may bite to get their point across. These are normal traits of childhood development.

The responsibility of the early childhood teacher is to eliminate as many of these accidents as possible. There are usually more accidents and injuries in the toddler classrooms due to the unsteady nature of one- and two-year-old children, but accidents can happen at any age level of the childcare program. These accidents can happen in the classroom, in the bathroom, and especially on the playground. In order to prevent unnecessary injuries, there are essential policies that must be in place in a quality childcare program.

One of the first steps toward ensuring a safe learning environment is to make sure that the facility and the materials are in good repair and appropriate for the children. For example, if the facility is in disrepair (e.g., ripped window screens, a broken toilet seat, or a sharp plastic edge on the playground slide), then children have a greater risk of getting injured.

If a toy or classroom material gets broken during the course of the school day, it should be removed from play until the piece can be repaired and is no longer a safety risk. The outdoor environment can be just as big of a risk. For example, if the sidewalk into the school is especially slick from ice in the wintertime or if the playground has a wasp nest, then children are at risk for injury.

Classroom furnishings need to be the appropriate size for young children. Tall shelves in the toddler classroom will encourage young children to climb and possibly fall off of the shelving. A stack of four or five child-sized chairs in the corner of the classroom can easily fall on top of a young toddler. When the teachers and the program administrator set up the environment to eliminate these types of accidents, it creates a safer experience for the children.

Medication

Childcare programs can also prevent unnecessary accidents by having strict procedures regarding medication. If your child must receive medication at school, the medication should be stored in a locked box out of the reach of all the children in the facility. Medication should only be dispensed from its original container that specifically describes the dose and the time increments at which the medication can be safely dispensed.

Your child's name must be on the medication to ensure that it is given to the correct child. You should fill out written and signed instructions stating when the child needs to take the medication next, how much he or she needs, and your consent for the medication to be offered to your child. Strict medication policies ensure that your child gets the proper dose of the medication and the specific medication that you provided. Make sure that the childcare program has these procedures laid out in the parent handbook.

Allergies

Staff may have to assist with injuries or an emergency situation when working in a childcare program. One of the scariest emergencies that many teachers face is an allergic reaction. Severe allergic reactions can occur to young children who have a diagnosed allergy or can happen for the first time while the child is in childcare. If your child has a diagnosed allergy, it is critical to ask the program in advance what type of precautions the center can offer.

Is the center peanut free or nut free? Is the staff trained to administer an EpiPen? Can your child bring an alternate lunch to avoid potential food allergies in the classroom? If your child is still a toddler and does not understand why he cannot have the same foods as the other children in the classroom, does the program have an emergency plan if he ingests a food that could cause him to stop breathing? There also needs to be an emergency plan in place during the summer months for a child who is allergic to bee or wasp stings.

If your child has a life-threatening allergy, it is essential to notify the childcare program as soon as you tour and begin to consider the school. Make sure that the appropriate measures are in place to keep your child safe at all times.

Weather Emergencies and Natural Disasters

Not all emergency situations are medical by nature. Quality early childhood programs must also be prepared for weather emergencies and natural disasters. Every childcare program should have an established emergency plan in the event of a fire, tornado, earthquake, or flood. This plan should include a relocation site in the event that it is no longer safe to stay inside the facility. Many centers are also adding a lockdown procedure to their emergency plan to ensure the safety of all the children in the building.

These emergency plans are typically required by the licensing regulations, but they need to be shared with enrolled families prior to an emergency. If the center has an off-site relocation spot for emergencies, then the families need to know where the relocation site is. When an emergency occurs, does the center have a way to notify you through a local news station or by text message, or should each family expect a phone call from one of the staff members?

Along with establishing a plan for emergencies, the early childhood program must train the teachers on what to do during an emergency. This begins by providing first aid and CPR training to every staff member on a regular schedule. It is important to know how many staff members have CPR and first aid training.

Is there always someone in your child's classroom who knows first aid and CPR? Accreditations through organizations like NAEYC require that children never be left alone with a staff member who does not have CPR and first aid training in order to make sure that children never have to wait for emergency care when it is needed.

Other emergency training, like how to use an EpiPen or what to do in a natural disaster, gives the staff members the confidence to act quickly and efficiently when an emergency does occur. Finally, the children need training on emergencies as well. It is crucial for children to practice emergency drills on a regular basis so that they can remain as calm as possible during an actual emergency.

REDUCING THE SPREAD OF ILLNESS

One of the downfalls of group childcare is that when children begin attending a group setting, they will most likely get sick at some point. This downfall is outweighed by greater benefits like school readiness skills and children successfully learning to play together in groups. However, when your children are exposed to germs from other children, they will become sick.

Toddlers have a difficult time blowing their noses and washing their hands properly, so they frequently share their germs with their classmates. Children in childcare may get sick more than children who have individualized care, but over time, we see those same children build up immunity to illness. When the same children begin Kindergarten, they typically miss fewer days than the children who had private care during their preschool years.

At one point or another, young children all get sick. In a high-quality early childhood program, the teachers attempt to keep the environment free from germs and teach the children the skills they need to eliminate sharing their germs with others. There are many licensing regulations that monitor illness in group care, how to clean a childcare program properly, and how to prepare food to avoid foodborne illnesses in group-care settings. These are all policies that should be in the parent and staff handbooks for an early childhood program.

When you tour a childcare program, ask about the program's illness policy before enrolling your child. When are children sent home with contagious illnesses? What constitutes a contagious illness? What is the temperature at which a child is considered to have a fever? How long after a contagious illness must your child stay home before returning to the classroom? Although these procedures can be frustrating for working families that need daily childcare, it is important to remember that these procedures also keep your children from getting sick when another child must stay home to recuperate.

Fevers

Many childcare programs follow the American Academy of Pediatrics' recommendations for contagious illnesses and a fever of 101 degrees as reasons to stay home from childcare, but other programs have stricter policies. It is important for you to know in advance when you could receive a phone call to come and get your child if she is not feeling well. It is also important to know if you must collect your child within a certain time frame once the childcare program has contacted you.

Immunizations

Does the childcare program have a policy on required immunizations? This is a controversial topic for many families; however, state laws require many childcare programs to have an up-to-date certificate of immunization for each child or a statement from the doctor explaining that the child's religious beliefs require that he or she not receive immunizations. It is important to know what your program does when your child's current immunization certificate runs out. If it expires, will your child be asked to leave the program if the immunizations are not renewed?

Many families are also curious about the immunizations of the staff. Are the staff required or encouraged to have specific immunizations in order to work with young children? Are they provided flu shots each year? These are questions you are free to ask the program administrator, but remember that immunizations are a personal choice. Employees and families enrolled in the program may choose not to immunize. If that is the case, then the childcare program should keep that information confidential for the children and the employees.

Hand Washing

The frontline defense against germs in any childcare program is hand washing! This is an essential part of every day in the early childhood classroom. Many states even list when children and staff are required to wash their hands in their licensing regulations.

The most common requirements include washing of hands upon arrival at the childcare program, before and after mealtime, before and after diapering, after toileting, and after sneezing or coughing. Your child should also be asked to wash her hands after playing in a community activity like the water table or a sensory tub.

As soon as children are able to stand at the sink with assistance, they should start to learn the process of hand washing. Then as they become more independent, they can wash their hands whenever needed. Teachers should encourage children to wet their hands first and then use soap to wash both the front and back of their hands before rinsing. Although all teachers understand the importance of washing hands, it is often forgotten when the classroom gets hectic. When you tour or observe a classroom, make sure that hand washing is second nature to the classroom staff and the children.

Diapering and Toileting

Diapering and toileting can easily spread germs if childcare providers are not careful to follow a sanitary procedure. Many childcare programs will actually post diapering procedures in the room so that even substitute teachers can remember how to keep the changing area sanitary at all times.

The changing area must be cleaned and sanitized before and after a diaper change. The staff must dispose of soiled diapers in a trashcan that is separate from the rest of the classroom, and both the child and the provider must wash their hands before returning to the classroom's normal activities.

The teacher should be wearing gloves while cleaning the child, and he or she should throw away the gloves when disposing of the soiled diaper. Your child should never be left alone on a changing table, so the provider needs to collect all the items needed before placing him on the changing table.

Toilet training a young child can be more complicated than changing a diaper. The childcare provider needs to wear gloves in order to assist the child, but the provider needs to allow the child to be as independent as possible. Both the provider and the child need to wash their hands immediately after toileting.

Depending on the child's accuracy, the provider may also need to clean and sanitize the toilet after the child is finished. It is much more sanitary for a childcare program to use small toilets than to have families bring in individual potty chairs. Due to the porous material that potty chairs are made of, it can be much more challenging to clean them properly multiple times per day than a typical ceramic toilet.

Cleaning Classroom Areas

During diapering, mealtimes, or when cleaning toys, quality early childhood programs have procedures for both cleaning and sanitizing the classroom areas. Cleaning is removing dirt, and it is done with soap and water. Sanitizing is killing germs, and it is usually done with a cleaning component like bleach. Areas that come in contact with many germs like diaper changing tables, meal areas, and toys that have been mouthed by young children need the opportunity to be cleaned and sanitized, possibly several times per day.

Childcare programs that use sanitizers made of bleach must make sure that the bleach to water ratio is safe and will not hurt the teachers' or the children's skin. Bleach should always be stored out of the reach of young children. Outdoor equipment, like the playground, should be rinsed off with water occasionally, and outdoor water tables should be emptied and refilled frequently.

Handling Food and Bottles

Finally, if a childcare program is going to provide meals to your child, the staff must prevent illness by handling food items appropriately. Hot items need to be served warm or hot, and cold items need to be served cool. Once these foods enter the room temperature range, then they are typically not fit to serve anymore. This is also true with baby bottles.

Once a bottle has been out of the refrigerator or warmed, it is only able to be served to an infant for one hour. After that, the formula or milk is at risk for spoilage. When childcare providers are preparing and serving food, they should wash their hands and then wear gloves. Many preschools have family style meals where your child can pass the bowl around the table and serve herself. This is appropriate as long as the children are using a serving spoon to prevent the food from being repeatedly touched.

Aside from illness and injury, there are several other health and safety issues that you should consider when looking for a childcare program.

HEALTHY MEALS

Childcare programs have the option to provide the meals for the children or have the families prepare and send a meal for each child. Regardless of who provides the meal, your childcare program may still be responsible for what the child eats during mealtime. Many states have regulations telling early childhood programs the serving sizes and the meal components that must be offered at each meal.

If you do not send all the food required, then it is the childcare program's responsibility to supplement the meal. If the program does provide meals to the children, remember that it is extremely difficult to provide meals that satisfy the preferences of every family.

The key requirements for the center are to include the necessary meal groups (protein, vegetables, fruits, etc.) in the required portion size. The program may be able to make substitutions for allergies, but that may be a responsibility of the family. Childcare programs typically select foods that are considered to be "child friendly." This usually means that the children can eat the food independently, the foods do not pose any choking hazards, and they are foods that young children enjoy. The early childhood program must balance a fine line of serving the healthiest foods possible while still serving foods that children will eat so that they do not go home hungry.

If you have specific food preferences, like an all-organic diet, then it will most likely be your responsibility to bring in those foods for your child while still meeting the required portions and food group requirements. When you tour childcare programs, ask to see the menu and review the food selections that will be served. If you would like to bring your own meals for your child, then ask the center what requirements you must follow.

SAFE SLEEP

If you are looking for infant care, then it is important to understand the principles of Safe Sleep. The American Academy of Pediatrics' "Safe Sleep" statement from 2011 recommends that all infants sleep on their backs in a crib with only a fitted sheet and a pacifier. The AAP does not recommend crib bumpers, stuffed animals, or loose clothing or bedding in the bed at any time. Infants should not be put to sleep with a bottle to prevent choking.

All childcare facilities are required to have cribs that were made for commercial use and meet the national regulations. An infant is not supposed to sleep in a swing, bouncy seat, or jumper for safety purposes. There are many laws about Safe Sleep for childcare programs throughout the United States, but they differ slightly from state to state. Some states may allow a tight blanket in the bed with the child, while others may not. *It is important to make sure that any potential childcare programs know and understand the Safe Sleep policies.*

If your child has colic, acid reflux, or a medical condition that discourages the child from sleeping flat on his or her back, then it is important to provide doctor documentation for the childcare providers to follow different instructions. Once your child sleeps on a mat, then he will be able to safely sleep with a blanket or a favorite stuffed animal.

SMOKE-FREE CAMPUS

Another question that you may ask yourself when selecting a childcare program is whether the childcare program is on a smoke-free campus. More and more childcare programs are making the decision to ban smoking on the property. An employer does not have the right to tell its employees that he or she cannot smoke; however, a child care program can significantly reduce the amount of smoke that children are exposed to each day by asking staff and families not to smoke on the property. This also reduces the opportunity for your children to watch adults smoking.

Every state sets different requirements for healthy and safe childcare programs, so some of these procedures may be required in your area while others may be recommended practices. It is challenging to find every recommended practice in place, but it is important to ask questions during the selection process (such as "Is this a smoke-free facility?") so that you have the opportunity to decide which characteristics are the most important to you.

Ultimately, you want to know that your child is safe and healthy, even when you are apart. Select the childcare program that you believe will best care for your child in a healthy and safe environment.

- Is there a first aid kit in each room?
- Is there at least one person per classroom with CPR and first aid training?
- Do classrooms maintain low student-to-teacher ratios?
- What is the maximum number of children in each classroom?
- What is the center's policy on administering medication?
- Are healthy meals served to the children?
- What is the program's illness policy?
- Does the program have an emergency and disaster plan in place that includes natural disasters and relocation if necessary?

FIVE

Quality Early Childhood Educators

As a parent, it is fabulous to find a childcare program with a respected accreditation, with a beautiful facility, and with the hours of operation that you need, but ultimately, you are leaving your child with the *people* who work in the program, not the building or the accreditation. The teachers and the administrators are the most significant part of the childcare selection process.

You may be able to find a highly recommended center; however, if you do not feel comfortable leaving your child with his or her teacher, then you will not end up staying enrolled in the program for very long.

The staff members make the program what it is. They are the backbone of the school's success. For parents who are upset that they cannot stay at home with their children during these early years, it is essential that the family trust the childcare provider and the program administrator in order to establish feelings of safety and comfort. There are several factors that families should consider when thinking about quality early childhood professionals:

- Quality early childhood teachers: education, experience, and relationships
- Quality administrators
- Teacher turnover
- Does the program support the staff?

QUALITY EARLY CHILDHOOD TEACHERS

Today's early childhood professional looks very different from thirty years ago. When early childhood classrooms first began, they were considered to be group babysitting experiences for working families. The health and safety of the children was the primary focus. These classrooms often attracted caregivers who had previous experience babysitting, but there were no formal demands like specific training or a desired number of years of experience working in the field.

Now, early childhood education is the *foundation* for a quality elementary school experience. Preschool appeals not only to working families, but also to families that want their children to be in a large social setting before Kindergarten or families whose children have a developmental delay. There is also increasing pressure on families and teachers to have children prepared for the academic demands of Kindergarten, which become more challenging each year.

Early childhood educators need to secure the health and safety of the children in their classrooms, and they also need to help them develop social skills, learn to follow directions, learn self-help skills, develop pre-academic skills, and help the children feel safe and loved each day they are at school. This means that teachers need far more training than in years past.

Teachers may need experience as an assistant teacher prior to moving up to a leadership position like a lead teacher. The teachers must also develop strong relationships with the children and their families in order to help children meet developmental goals at home and at school.

Teacher Education

There are many different ways that a childcare provider can receive education about his or her field. Many states do not require any higher education in order to work in a childcare program; however, they do require that all childcare providers receive annual training about working with young children.

Professional development trainings for early childhood educators cover topics like child development, developmentally appropriate curriculum, professionalism, health and safety, parent and community partnerships, and working with children with special needs.

Most childcare providers must receive fifteen to twenty-five hours of training per year in order to meet the state licensing requirements for professional development. Some childcare programs may require their staff members to attend more than the minimum amount of training, or they may bring in guest speakers to teach their staff on specific areas of interest. It is always helpful to know what type of training that your child's teachers are receiving, so don't hesitate to ask!

Child Development Associate

There are also formal degrees that early childhood educators can obtain that are specific to the field of early childhood education. The Child Development Associate (CDA) is a nationally recognized early childhood education credential offered through the Council for Professional Recognition in Washington, DC. CDA candidates must complete 120 hours of formal training and 480 hours of classroom observations before receiving their credential.

The training hours for a CDA are equivalent to approximately two college courses, and candidates can focus their observations toward the preschool classroom or the infant/toddler classroom. Candidates must also compile a professional portfolio, take an examination covering the content of the formal training, and have a CDA specialist complete a formal observation in the classroom while the candidate is working with young children.

The CDA is considered an introductory degree in the field of early childhood education, but it still provides very specific training and field experience to prepare new teachers for a successful experience in the classroom.

Higher Education Degrees

Most colleges and universities now offer several different options for prospective teachers looking for a degree in early childhood education. The most common degrees include child development, early childhood education, and early childhood special education.

A child development degree typically focuses on developmental milestones of the child from prenatal development through adolescence. This degree also focuses on what circumstances lead to normal development and what scenarios could make development more challenging for a typical child.

Early childhood education and early childhood special education are teacher education programs that provide the student with a degree and the ability to apply for a teacher's certificate. Both of these programs focus on child development as well as quality curriculum for the early childhood classroom. The early childhood education degree focuses both on children with and without special needs, but the early childhood special education degree provides the teacher with a great deal of education on how to meet the needs of young children with special needs.

The requirements for teacher's certificates vary from state to state, but these degrees typically allow the teacher to obtain a teacher's certificate for children from birth through the early primary grades. These majors are offered at an associate's degree, a bachelor's degree, or a master's degree level in the field of early childhood education. Students with an associate's degree will probably not qualify to pursue a teacher's certificate, but many early childhood programs do not require a teacher's certificate for their teachers.

Although they are not the same as early childhood education degrees, many accreditations will allow a teacher to hold a related degree. In order to be considered a related degree, the degree must provide some training on child development and working with young children. Degrees that are considered to be related to early childhood can include elementary education, psychology, sociology, family studies, special education, or other degree programs that include child development or early education.

When a teacher holds a related degree, he or she may still need some additional training in the field of early childhood education. For example, a teacher with a degree in elementary education may understand the general principles of child development and how to create curriculum for the classroom, but the teacher may need some training on what activities are developmentally appropriate for children who are two and three years old. This additional training can be included in the teacher's annual training requirements for the state.

Teacher Experience

It is critical for a teacher to be knowledgeable about early childhood education, but knowledge is only one characteristic of a successful teacher. It is also essential that every teacher has *experience* working with children between the ages of birth and five years.

Although learning about children's behaviors can benefit a teacher, it is nothing like the hands-on experience of being in a classroom with twenty preschoolers.

Children are creative, energetic little beings who can surprise you every day, and experienced teachers have been in the classroom with these surprises and have learned how to handle each situation they have encountered. It is important to ask if your child's teacher has previous experience, but there are several types of experience to consider.

First, it is important to find out if the teacher has experience in the field of early childhood education. Other fields of education focus on the product that students create, but in early childhood, teachers focus on the *process* of learning, not the final results. Children learn through play in early childhood classrooms instead of sitting still for long periods of time. These are key points with which an early childhood educator should be familiar.

Second, it is important to ask about the teacher's experience at the preschool program that you are viewing. Because the field of early childhood education is not a high-paying industry, there is a relatively high rate of turnover. It is helpful to find out if the teacher has a long tenure with the school you are considering.

If not, it does not mean that the teacher will leave quickly, but if the teacher has been at the program at least a year then he or she has some tenure and should be familiar with the school policies and procedures. This will be a huge help when you need to ask questions.

Third, it is also important to ask how long the teacher has been working with the age group of the classroom. There are huge differences between working in the infant room and teaching preschool. If a teacher is new to the age group with which he or she is working, it is important that the co-teacher has experience with the age group to acclimate the new teacher.

Relationships

A high-quality teacher is not outstanding without the ability to develop relationships. This is the piece of the equation that allows a parent or caregiver to leave a newborn in someone else's care or gives a grandparent the peace of mind to drive to work without worrying about a grandchild.

Exceptional teachers must develop quality relationships with students, families, and their coworkers in order to serve the children in their care. These traits are harder to check off of a list, but most families can identify this aspect once they observe a teacher in the classroom. Is the teacher warm, sensitive, and comforting to the students?

This doesn't mean that the teacher must hug the children continuously, but when the children are upset, can the teacher calm them down? Do the children appear happy to see the teacher, and does the teacher respond in the same way?

Does the teacher invite parents and family members into the classroom to see what the children are learning and to spend time with the children? Does the teacher participate with the children in activities instead of standing back to watch? Does the teacher talk to the children when he or she is in the classroom instead of primarily talking to the other adults?

The teacher also needs to work hard to develop a relationship with each family. This means establishing open, two-way communication. Does the teacher send home newsletters or e-mail the families with updates of what is going on in the classroom each week? Does the teacher contact the family when he or she has concerns about the child being ill or having a difficult time at school?

When considering an early childhood program for your child, ask the teacher how he or she communicates with the families. This way you know if you should expect phone calls, e-mails, printed newsletters, or parent-teacher conferences.

It is also important to see if the teacher values your goals and priorities for your child. Most teachers set developmental goals for the students in their classrooms. These can be academic goals, independence skills, social skills, or other developmental goals.

When the teacher sets these goals, it is very important that he or she ask what you feel is the most important for your child. If a parent desperately wants her preschooler to write his name before starting Kindergarten or if the family of a toddler is working hard to toilet train their two-year-old, it is important that the teacher knows this information and partners with the families to achieve these goals.

Finally, it is essential that a quality childcare provider enjoys his or her job! Just like any other profession, if you don't like your job, then you are less motivated to do your job well. The field of education is exactly the same, except that educators are dealing with far more valuable merchandise!

Children deserve to come to school every day and see a teacher who is happy to see them and happy to be there. Teachers who

enjoy their job stay in the profession much longer and further reduce teacher turnover. Also, teachers who are happy to do their jobs
typically go out of their way to help each student learn. As a parent,
that is the type of teacher you want spending the day with your
child!

QUALITY ADMINISTRATORS

The director or the administrator of a childcare program sets the
standard for how all the educators must conduct themselves. Often,
the director is either focused on the business of the childcare program or the education of the childcare program. Whichever of these
components that the director values the most is often the component that is stressed at the center.

Recently there has been a trend for larger early childhood programs to hire an education director to focus on supervising the
teachers and to have a business director that focuses on the management issues of the program. Small childcare programs may not have
this luxury. The administrator of a smaller early childhood education program may have to wear both hats—the education specialist
and the business manager.

Childcare program directors often have a long list of job responsibilities attached to their positions. They must:

- supervise staff
- evaluate job performance
- hire new staff members
- set employee schedules
- supervise professional development of staff members
- step into the classroom when needed
- advertise the childcare program
- offer tours to prospective families
- complete enrollment paperwork
- maintain required documentation on children and staff
- supervise state and national regulations
- establish school policies

Additionally, they must maintain relationships with all the program families, answer questions and concerns of families, moderate
disagreements between staff members, maintain the facility and
grounds, collect tuition, supervise payroll, order supplies for the

program, write grants, organize fundraisers, and fill in wherever needed.

With the wide variety of tasks that directors must complete, it is essential for quality administrators to have several key characteristics: education and experience in the field of early childhood education, experience in administration, business experience (or business support), and personal relationships with the staff and families enrolled.

Education and Experience as a Classroom Teacher

In order to supervise and mentor the classroom teachers effectively, it is *essential that the childcare program director have education and experience in early childhood education*. A degree in early childhood education is very important because it trains a program director on typical and atypical child development.

Many families approach the program director to ask questions like, "Is it normal for my child to . . .?" or, "How do I get my child to stop . . .?" These questions are rooted in child development.

Many early childhood programs provide parent education events or bring in guest speakers for community education. Even if the director is not the speaker at these activities, it is important that he or she be knowledgeable on the topic to facilitate discussions and answer questions after the presenter is gone.

When a teacher approaches a family about concerns with a child's behavior, the director is typically involved in these conversations. If he or she is well versed in early childhood education, then the director is able to support the teacher's opinion and explain to the family why the program has concerns and what steps the family should take next.

A director will also need to mentor the teachers in the childcare program. One of the largest challenges for most teachers is classroom behavior management or dealing with difficult behaviors. The director must have formal training on behavior management and challenging behaviors in order to coach the teachers through difficult situations.

Classroom experience is just as important to a director's skill set as a degree in the field. Books and laws can tell you that one adult is capable of taking care of six toddlers, but unless the director has had that experience, he or she does not fully understand the hard work and patience the staff must have to work in a toddler classroom. A director who has worked "in the trenches" with children and families can show a great deal of empathy to the teaching staff, and staff members respond well to empathy.

When a teacher works in the classroom, he or she develops tricks of the trade in order to best serve the children. These are not skills that are taught in textbooks, but they are important skills to learn in order to be a teacher. A director with experience in the classroom will be able to mentor classroom teachers more effectively if he or she can share the strategies that worked for him or her.

Experience as an Administrator

When you consider a childcare program, it is important to see if the director has experience as an administrator. Not every amazing classroom teacher is meant to be in a management position. Being an administrator requires many teachers to step out of their comfort zones by supervising and disciplining coworkers, having challenging conversations with staff or enrolled families, making decisions that cannot make everyone happy, and spending long hours at work in order to ensure the program's success.

Some teachers were made for administration and can easily step into these job obligations, but others may need to train under an experienced administrator before taking a top leadership role for the school.

After a full school year of experience, a new director has typically encountered most of the challenges that he or she will have to deal with year after year; however, there will always be surprises. There may be rough winter storms one year that cause the director to evaluate if the school should stay open or if it would be better for staff safety to close the program for the day. These are the tough decisions that will never make everyone happy.

After navigating a few of these scenarios, a skilled administrator will determine a policy to guide the decision-making process, and then he or she will know how to handle the situation again in the future.

Business Experience or Support

When a teacher receives a degree in early education, it does *not* include any training on staff supervision, human resources, budgeting, payroll, marketing, or recruitment. These are often the areas that educators struggle with most when they initially accept a leadership position. If the new administrator does not have a business background or experience in nonprofit management, then frequently the owner or administrative board for the program will train the director how to budget for the center, run payroll, and order the necessary supplies.

There may be a training period before the new director takes on these jobs permanently, or it may be the job of the owner or administrative board to perform the basic business functions of the childcare program. It is harder for a new director to get training on staff supervision and hiring new employees. Administrators usually learn these skills in the field.

Once a director has hired several staff members who quit soon after they were hired, then he or she learns what to look for on employee applications in order to avoid these situations in the future. The key for a director without any business experience is to have an advisor or an advisory panel that can give trusted insight for business decisions.

Personal Relationships with Families and Staff

The program director is the model for customer service throughout the childcare center. Each family wants someone to listen to their concerns, their joys, and their daily struggles. When the families feel that they have this type of relationship within the center, they are more likely to be content. It is essential for the director to learn the names of children, the names of the families, and the concerns of the parents. These details make a huge difference to the families whose children are enrolled in the program.

When you select a childcare program for your child, you want to make sure that the teachers and director know how special your child is and that you have a voice in how your child is cared for each day. This is why a director must have a relationship with every family in the program. The families are more comfortable coming to speak with the director if they know that the director knows who their children are and that the director is willing to listen.

It is also essential for the director to have strong relationships with the program staff. The administrator's job as a supervisor is to be a cheerleader for every staff member. The staff members need to feel supported, because if they do not, they will leave to go to a childcare program where they *do* feel supported. This goes beyond simply knowing all of the families; the director needs to make an effort to know details about the staff.

It is important for the administrator to know the teachers' strengths and weaknesses, not only for evaluations, but also to encourage the staff members to excel and to find the most compatible teaching teams. The director is the coach of the team, and he or she must do everything possible to prepare and encourage the team members to do their best.

TEACHER TURNOVER

Early childhood education has one of the highest teacher turnover rates out of the entire education field. There are several reasons for this higher rate of turnover. First, professionals in the field of early childhood education are still paid significantly less than any other branch of education. When a teacher receives a degree or a teacher's certificate in early childhood education, it is often tempting to leave and pursue a job in a higher paying job market.

Another reason for turnover is that many teachers become frustrated with the level of respect and professionalism offered to most early childhood educators. Research has shown us the importance of early childhood education, but there is still a stigma that childcare providers do not need to be educated or professionals in order to do their jobs. When an early childhood education professional continues to be compared to a babysitter, he or she may become too frustrated with the career path to stay in the classroom.

Working in childcare is a physically demanding job. Teachers must pick up children throughout the day. They must sit down on and get up from the floor repeatedly. They must run after children on the playground, sit in short chairs only inches off the floor, and sit in bean bag chairs to read children stories. Since working in an early childhood classroom can be exhausting, many teachers decide not to spend their entire career in this classroom setting.

Finally, many teachers leave the field of early childhood education due to burnout. Early childhood education is unique from other areas of education because teachers work with children *and* families each day.

Teachers become parent educators and give families techniques to work with their children at home. They nurture and teach children with and without special needs in the classroom each day. They spend their own time and money outside of the classroom to prepare lessons and provide materials for the children. They must continue their own education in order to serve their students best.

Many teachers believe that educating young children is their mission in life, so the demands of the job do not bother them. Other teachers can offer this time and dedication for a phase of their career but then desire to move on to another career path. With all of these reasons for teacher turnover, it is easy to see why your child may have multiple teachers during the course of a school year.

Generational Traits of Teachers

Another factor that can affect teacher turnover in your child's classroom is the generational traits of the teachers. We know that many Traditionalists and Baby Boomers value serving the majority of their career in the same school, but Generation X and Millennials have a slightly different view on career commitment.

Generation X members do not believe there is a required time period to stay at most jobs. Many of these teachers will only stay one or two years in a particular school before moving to a school that can offer them better benefits, higher pay, or a more family-friendly environment.

Millennials are willing to stay longer in a job setting than Gen Xers if they have a positive work environment and some flexibility with their jobs. Overall, the social standard for teaching positions is for teachers to stay in increments of one year so that the students may finish the school year without interruption. Many early childhood professionals will follow this rule in preschools that follow a typical school year calendar, but for year-round childcare programs, there is no socially accepted time period to resign and teachers may come and go throughout the year.

Primary Caregivers

When selecting a childcare program for your child, it is important to ask questions about the classroom teachers. Always ask how long the teacher has been in the field and how long the teacher has been with that particular school. Another important question, especially in infant and toddler classrooms, is whether the classroom has primary caregivers.

A primary caregiver is an early childhood professional who is primarily responsible for a small group of children in the classroom. For example, in an infant room with eight children and two teachers, one teacher would be primarily responsible for four of the children in the classroom.

That teacher would learn the infants' feeding cues, how they want to be put to sleep, and how to soothe the children. The other teacher in the classroom may still assist with those children, but the primary caregiver would establish a strong bond with the children in his or her care. This style of caregiving is used not only to establish strong attachment at a young age, but also to keep the teachers invested in the children in their classrooms.

At the same time, a change in a primary caregiver can be harder for a child to deal with than when one member of a teaching team changes.

Permanent Classroom Staff and Center Floaters

When it comes to teacher turnover, there is a difference in consistency between permanent classroom staff and between center "floaters" whose main job may be to give breaks and fill in as substitute teachers. Many centers hire new staff members to be floaters and move them to a permanent classroom placement once the administrator has seen how the staff members work with the children and families.

Many new employees may not understand the demands of a job in early education or may think because they enjoy playing with children that they are suited for a job in childcare. The director's priority is to keep more consistency with the primary teachers in each classroom.

Children can deal with the occasional inconsistency of a substitute or someone different giving the teacher a break for lunch, but the consistency of the main teachers in the classroom is much more important.

DOES THE PROGRAM SUPPORT THE STAFF?

The best method an administrator has to reduce staff turnover is to support the staff. Obviously many staff members would ultimately love to have a higher paying salary, but the childcare program many not have the financial means to offer that. Instead, directors need to be more creative to find ways to take care of their teaching staff. Childcare programs that offer their employees health insurance (medical, dental, etc.) typically have lower turnover rates than those that do not offer these benefits.

Many childcare programs may not be able to offer higher pay, but they offer a childcare discount to all of their employees. Early childhood professionals can be enticed by reduced tuition rates and the ability to work in the same building as their own children. Other benefits might include paid time off and providing free professional development training to staff members.

Due to limited budgets, many directors must think out of the box in order to offer incentives to their teaching staff. For example, many administrators may enlist the support of the families and encourage parents to show expressions of staff appreciation like potlucks or needed teacher supplies. The program may choose to encourage dedicated staff members with incentives like employee of the month or prime parking spots.

Some centers use staff competitions to develop team collaboration and to use effectively the small amount of money they have for teacher appreciation. The key to all of these efforts is to make sure that quality teachers feel encouraged and appreciated so they will stay in their positions for an extended period of time.

- Are the staff members nurturing and inviting to the children and the families?
- Does the director have training (a degree) and experience in the field?
- Do the teachers have training (a degree or certification) and experience in the field?
- How long has the teacher been with the center? With that age group?
- Do the teachers/staff receive annual training in the field?

SIX

Quality Curriculum and the Developmentally Appropriate Environment

When you ask most families what they are seeking from their children's childcare program, many will start by saying that they want a healthy and safe childcare program. The next most common answer is that families desire to find a childcare center that prepares their children for Kindergarten and offers a school-readiness curriculum. "School readiness" means different things to different people. Many early childhood professionals believe that "school readiness" means the children are socially prepared for Kindergarten and have the language and independence skills to learn what the teachers will begin teaching in the new school year.

Families may believe that "school readiness" means their children enter Kindergarten with the abilities to write their names and identify the letters of the alphabet. Early childhood educators are responsible for teaching content in multiple areas of development: health and safety skills, self-help and independence skills, language development, fine and gross motor development, sensory skills, problem solving, and pre-academic skills.

All of these skills (e.g., social skills, independence, and academic knowledge) must be taught in a classroom environment that is appropriate to the development level of each child. The teacher must keep the children in the classroom interested and offer a variety of learning experiences. When you begin considering childcare programs for your child, you must identify which classrooms offer a quality curriculum and provide a classroom environment that is appropriate for all the children who attend.

AREAS OF CONTENT

- *Health and safety skills* allow the child to function in the classroom by reducing the risk of injury or illness. Children in the early childhood classroom must learn about the toilet-training process. They must learn about hand washing as soon as they are able to stand independently. Toddlers and preschool students learn how to brush their teeth after eating and how to keep their food on their own plates at mealtime.
- The teachers also educate the families on the importance of children getting the proper amount of sleep, getting regular checkups with a pediatrician, and getting recommended immunizations to prevent illness. Even in the infant room, the teachers begin practicing emergency drills with the children to teach them what to do in an emergency situation. The teachers are also trained on first aid, CPR, and how to administer medication in order to provide a safe classroom for the students.
- *Self-help skills* are skills that help a child be more independent on a daily basis. This includes learning to eat, use the restroom independently, and dress/undress independently. When teachers plan self-help skills for the classroom it can include skills like using a zipper, brushing hair, using a fork at mealtime, or toilet training.
- *Language development* includes understanding what someone says to you and using verbal and nonverbal skills to express yourself to others. Infants and young toddlers may demonstrate these skills by crying when they need assistance. The teacher may then set a goal for that child to use a one-word phrase to express a need or want. Preschoolers may be learning how to have a conversation or answer an in-depth question.
- *Gross motor skills* are large muscle activities. We see children achieve many gross motor skills at a young age when they roll over, sit up, learn to crawl, and learn to walk. Older children will be mastering skills like running, walking up and down stairs, and skipping. Teachers must provide gross motor play

each day in the classroom, not only so that young children master skills, but so that children also learn the importance of exercise.

- *Fine motor skills* are activities done with the hands and fingers like playing with Legos, stringing beads, cutting with scissors, drawing with crayons, snapping fingers, buttoning, and writing with a pencil. Gross motor skills develop before fine motor skills. Once the fine motor skills begin to develop, teachers must provide activities that allow children to develop hand strength and master intricate movements.

- *Sensory activities* give young children the opportunity to learn by tasting, smelling, touching, hearing, and seeing. Children get to play with clay, finger paint, and taste test different kinds of apples. Most of the classroom music and art activities can be described as sensory experiences. The early childhood classroom should be set up so that children can touch and experience all the materials, but the planned sensory activities will single out a specific experience for all of the children to try.

- *Problem-solving skills* occur when the teacher does not immediately come to the child's aid. Children must learn how to resolve a disagreement with a classmate or repair a block tower that repeatedly falls down. Teachers can encourage problem solving by asking the children questions about possible solutions and by creating a classroom that allows children to make mistakes.

- *Pre-academic skills* include skills from math, reading, writing, and the sciences. Pre-math skills include sorting, classifying, measuring, and counting. Pre-reading skills include identifying letters, learning letter sounds, learning environmental print, and learning basic sight words like the names of classmates and family members. Writing skills include learning to hold a crayon, coloring, tracing, writing letters, and then writing the child's name. Science skills include learning about the weather, the seasons, animals and their homes, and making predictions.

All early childhood classrooms offer curriculum to their students. Even infant and toddler rooms provide curriculum. The curriculum for a classroom of infants will look very different from the curriculum for a classroom of preschool students; however, infant teachers still plan sensory experiences, early art activities, language and preliteracy activities, and motor skill activities for all the children in the classroom.

When you tour an infant or toddler classroom, *you should still see evidence of teacher planning just like in the preschool classroom.* Just remember that infant and toddler classrooms must devote a larger percentage of their day to caring for the children's basic needs.

QUALITY CURRICULUM

Quality early childhood curriculum is not packaged the same way that elementary school curriculum is presented. Elementary schools may use curriculum produced by a national publisher that includes activities for reading, handwriting, math, science, and other content. This curriculum is set up for the teacher to present the learning content and for students to sit and listen to new information. Quality early childhood curriculum is more play based and utilizes learning centers as well as small-group activities led by a classroom teacher.

The curriculum should include content areas like literacy, writing, math, science, fine motor development, sensory activities, dramatic play, blocks, music, art, and technology. When you observe this curriculum in the classroom, it will *not* include the teacher leading lessons in each of these curriculum areas every day. Instead, the teacher should have prepared the classroom to have hands-on learning materials that represent each of these curriculum subjects.

The students learn through exploring and playing with the materials. For very young classrooms, the children may learn through touching the materials, tasting them, listening to them, and observing what the materials look like. By preschool, the children may already know how to use the materials or they may use the materials to pretend that they represent something else. You should also see small-group activities that are more structured and led by an adult for a more specific learning objective.

Structured but Flexible

Children respond well to a structured and predictable classroom environment. Essential classroom routines like drop-off and pick-up, meals, naps, and diapering/toileting need to occur at regular intervals each day. Having a set schedule can create a sense of safety and security for each young child.

Children who are nervous about school or worry about being separated from their families can thrive with a schedule that allows them to know what to expect next during the day. At the same time, families and childcare providers need to understand that, even when a schedule is established, working with young children can mean the schedule must change based on the needs of the child. This means that each schedule needs to be structured yet flexible.

Flexible schedules still give the classroom an opportunity to expand on an activity when the children are in the midst of deep learning or it allows the classroom to adapt when the children need more individualized attention. Even when the teachers follow the needs of the children and spend some additional time on a certain activity, the sequence of the schedule still remains consistent.

Balance of Activities

With every activity that your child is offered in the early childhood classroom, he or she should also have an opportunity for balance. Children need an opportunity to learn to play independently, but they also need to learn how to play together in a group, large or small. Students need the opportunity to talk one-on-one with the teacher, but they also need the opportunity to learn how to speak with their peers.

The classroom needs to provide centers that allow children to be social (like the pretend play area or the block center), but the children also need areas that allow them to be quiet or work independently (like the book area, the writing center, or a designated quiet corner). The teacher should work with the children in small-group activities in order to find activities that meet the developmental needs of the children enrolled, but it is also important for each classroom to have a large group activity each day so that children can learn the social rules of being in a large group for a brief period of time.

All children need an opportunity to have daily outdoor play whenever possible, but it is important for the children to play indoors as well. As the teacher designs the classroom and the schedule, it is important to keep in mind the wide array of activities that must occur in order to meet the needs of all the students coming to school each day.

LANGUAGE-RICH ENVIRONMENT

A language-rich environment is a classroom or home that purposefully and continuously exposes young children to language in order to increase vocabulary and prepare students for conversation and reading skills. This type of classroom uses printed words, auditory stories, conversations, and storybooks to encourage learning. Teachers in language-rich classrooms read to the children daily, display a word wall, and label furniture and materials.

The teacher provides a diverse collection of books available to the children all day, offers writing materials to children throughout the day, and uses conversations between teachers and students and between students and peers as a teaching tool. The teacher should also involve families in the learning process by showing them how to use this model of learning in the home.

In an infant classroom, teachers may not offer children writing materials; however, the adults should be engaging in conversation with the children throughout the school day. If a very young child is only cooing or making blended sounds, then the teacher should pause to listen and consider that response as the infant's contribution to the conversation. Not only should a teacher talk to your child when he or she is sitting on the floor playing, but the teacher must begin conversations during diaper changes, feeding, and rocking a child to sleep.

Self-Talk and Parallel Talk

If there are two adults in the classroom, then they should model conversations between one another and speak to the children in the same manner, even if the children are not yet able to respond. Infant teachers must engage in self-talk and parallel talk. Self-talk is almost like a continual internal monologue by the teacher. "I am getting up off the floor now to get your bottle. I need to wait until your bottle is warm to take it out of the Crock-Pot. Now I need to get you a bib."

The teacher may feel awkward at first describing every action and movement that he or she makes in the classroom, but this process is offering small children a model of how adults use language. It is also beneficial because the teacher is exposing the child to new vocabulary as he or she speaks. Finally, self-talk can be a huge benefit to the teacher because many children can be soothed simply be hearing the voice of a trusted caregiver.

Parallel talk is similar to self-talk, but instead of the teacher describing his or her own actions, now the teacher is describing what the child is doing. "Are you upset? I can tell you are upset because you are crying and chewing on your fists. I think you want someone to pick you up."

Again, the sound of the teacher's voice can be an instant calming tool for many infants, but parallel talk offers a great deal of language stimulation to our youngest students. Finally, infants and toddlers should have access to books just like older students. The teacher should probably offer the student cloth books or board books that the child can touch, chew on, and explore. Despite the fact that the infant may not yet understand the purpose of the book, it is essential to expose the child to as many books as possible.

Print Recognition and Writing Opportunities

The preschool classroom can build on the conversation skills developed in the infant/toddler classroom by adding print recognition and writing opportunities to the classroom. Preschool students still need ample opportunities for adults to read books to them, but they also need to explore books on their own to see how to manipulate the book (e.g., how to hold the book, turn the pages, identify the pictures, etc.). There should be labels displayed throughout the preschool classroom like the infant/toddler classroom, but preschool teachers can begin using a word wall to focus on environmental print.

Environmental print refers to pictures that have an identified meaning for the child like a stop sign or the McDonald's logo. This is a child's first opportunity to understand that a picture or letters represent something else. Once children have been introduced to environmental print, then teachers can use the word wall for important names and key sight words that will be important to know when the children begin Kindergarten.

Open-Ended Questions

Along with self-talk and parallel talk, the preschool teacher needs to begin asking the children open-ended questions to develop a problem-solving mindset. Children are given many direct commands during the day like "put this away," "sit at the table," or "go wash your hands." The children must be able to comprehend the language in these directions, but these statements do not give children the opportunity to solve a problem or be creative.

When teachers and family members begin to ask children questions, then they are allowed to come up with their own thoughts. For example, instead of saying "Tell me your baby's name," the teacher can challenge the child to be more creative by asking, "Can you tell me about your baby? What does she like?" The teacher is not looking for a specific answer with these questions, and the children have the opportunity to tell stories and pretend as they answer.

Back and Forth Conversations

Another language skill that should be demonstrated in the preschool classroom is back and forth conversations. Teachers need to engage children in back and forth conversations, but children need to participate in these conversations with their friends also. Children will be able to have an extended conversation with a peer if they have observed and participated in this type of conversation with an adult. Adults need to show children how to stay on topic during the conversation and offer responses that are related to what the other person stated.

It is also essential for teachers to introduce new vocabulary each day. As a child's vocabulary increases and he or she knows more words, it makes it easier for that same child to later begin to write those words and read them.

When you observe in an early childhood classroom for your child, watch how the teacher communicates with the children. Does he or she ask questions? Does the teacher model appropriate conversations with a coworker to show the children how to engage in conversation? Does the infant teacher talk to the children even though the children cannot respond? Are words displayed throughout the classroom environment? These language development skills are an essential part of the learning environment, so they should be visible during the vast majority of the school day.

DEVELOPMENTALLY APPROPRIATE ENVIRONMENT

If a classroom or an activity is developmentally appropriate for a young child, then it is within the child's ability level to complete or understand the activity. An activity is not developmentally appropriate for a young child based on his or her age. Ability level can vary greatly even if all the children in the classroom are the same age. In a classroom full of four-year-olds, the teacher may have some students who have never seen a book before while others are beginning to read familiar words.

Planned activities for those two groups of students will be very different. The teacher will need to plan activities for some children to begin listening to stories for the first time and to learn how to handle the book. The other children may need an activity where they start to create their own books by drawing a picture and copying a simple word underneath the picture for a caption.

Experienced teachers have learned how to adapt materials so that many different children can use them and benefit from the activity. For example, a teacher can use a self-correcting activity to encourage independence in the classroom. This could be as simple as a letter-matching puzzle that allows children to match uppercase and lowercase letters together. The puzzle may be very appropriate for children who already know a large number of letters. The material could be self-correcting if each uppercase and lowercase pair is a different color. Even if the children do not know their letters yet, they can use the puzzle to match colors and get exposure to the alphabet letters.

You can see this same skill in the toddler classroom when a child uses a basic puzzle with as few as ten pieces. A two-year-old may be able to assemble the puzzle independently, but to help toddlers be more successful, the teacher may trace the outline of the puzzle pieces on the board so that younger toddlers have a map with which to match the shape of the pieces.

Some groups of children may be more advanced or more mature than the previous group. All teachers need to alter their plans to meet the needs of the children. This same principle applies when there are multiple preschool classrooms in the same childcare program. If there are three two-year-old classrooms in the same school, it is highly unlikely that all three classrooms need to work on the same skills at the same time.

One classroom may have excellent language skills, but the children need help developing their large muscle skills. Another classroom may enjoy reading books but have no children who are toilet trained yet. It is important that the teacher in each classroom creates a curriculum that meets the needs of the students enrolled. If the center uses a purchased curriculum, then it is important to ask the center director if the teachers can make modifications to the curricu-

lum based on the development of the students enrolled in the classroom.

THE CLASSROOM ENVIRONMENT

In a quality early childhood program, the children spend the most
time in the classroom. The classroom should be a warm and friendly environment that invites the children in to learn. There are also
several classroom traits that can make the environment more successful for the children. When you first view an infant/toddler or
preschool classroom, you should look to see if there are enough
materials for each child.

In the infant room, it is essential that every child has his or her
own crib and that there are enough swings, floor mats, and toys for
every child to play with when they are awake. In toddler and preschool classrooms, there should be more than enough toys for every
child in the classroom to use independently.

The classroom should not be set up so that every activity requires adult assistance. Every child in the room should be able to
explore the classroom and experiment with toys without having to
wait for a turn. Now, that does *not* mean that they can always get
the toys they prefer. It is okay for a child to wait for a specific toy,
but in the meantime, there should be other materials available.

Very popular toys should have duplicates in the classroom. If all
of the toddlers enjoy playing with a particular push toy, then it is a
wise decision for the classroom to have duplicates. If there is only
one of the most popular item in the room, that will often lead to
fighting. If all the toddlers want the same push toy, then the children may begin hitting or even biting to get the toy they want.
Classrooms can eliminate a lot of arguing and injuries with duplicate toys. When you tour a classroom, do you see some duplicate
toys offered in the classroom?

Centers

A quality early childhood classroom should be divided up into
centers so that like materials are located in the same areas. The
materials should not only be books, flat pictures, and worksheets.
Appropriate materials should include toys and activities that children can manipulate, take apart, touch, and explore. There should

be materials for building, pretend play, matching, sorting, creating, and listening.

Worksheets, like you would see in an elementary school classroom, should rarely be used in the preschool classroom. The purpose of art and writing in the toddler and preschool rooms is to experiment and create. This style of learning focuses on the process and not the product. Children will have many years of school, starting at Kindergarten, when the teacher is focused on the product that they create.

In preschool, the children should learn the steps to create and not worry about the end result. The art center should offer children a variety of materials like glue, paper, crayons, scissors, and glitter that allow children to be creative instead of creating a craft that must look the same for every child.

With a variety of centers and materials available to the children, then you should see very little wandering in the classroom. When you view the room, you should see children engaged in free play with the materials and possibly a teacher leading a small-group activity in the classroom. One of the best signs of a well-run classroom is to see all the children actively playing and enjoying the materials and their peers. When the teacher constantly puts new materials out in the room that peak the interests of the children, then the students stay engaged and behavior problems are reduced.

The Classroom Should Belong to the Children

It is also important for the children in the classroom to feel like the room belongs to them. The teacher can do this in several ways. First, every child should have a place in the classroom to put his or her personal belongings. Also, children can feel more at home in the classroom if they see familiar items.

Many teachers ask the families to bring in family pictures to put up in the classroom so the children will enjoy seeing people that they love. Other teachers might encourage parents to make a poster about the child that can be posted on the classroom walls. When children see these reminders of their personal lives, it can make the children feel safe and comforted in the classroom environment. These feelings of safety and comfort are also encouraged by seeing the same teachers' faces each day.

Classroom Observations

Most of these characteristics about the classroom structure, the language-rich environment, and the classroom centers can be observed during a brief observation of the classroom. When you go in to observe, remember to look for some of the following traits:

- Do the children seem familiar with the classroom schedule?
- Does the teacher assist the children during the transition?
- Does the teacher talk to the students?
- Do the adults model appropriate conversations, and do they ask the students questions?
- Do you see printed words throughout the classroom?
- Do the activities and materials seem appropriate for the children in the classroom?
- Are there enough materials for all of the children?
- Are children engaged with the materials, or are they wandering around the classroom?
- Does every child have an area for his or her own items in the classroom?

- Do the teachers speak to the infants and toddlers during playtime and during basic care routines (e.g., diapering, feeding, etc.)?
- Is there a lesson plan available for each classroom?
- Do children have indoor and outdoor play? Group and individual play? Quiet time when needed?
- Are there centers with different types of materials available (e.g., pretend-play materials, blocks, books, art materials, math materials, science activities, etc.)?
- Do the adults read to the children? Are there words displayed throughout the classroom?
- Are the teachers engaged with students instead of talking to one another?

SEVEN

Childcare for Children with Special Needs

Selecting childcare can be an overwhelming process for any family, but if your child has special needs, you may not feel safe leaving your child in many early childhood settings. Families of children with typical needs may use a school's accreditation or the reference of another parent to select a childcare program that meets the family's needs, but when you have a child with special needs (a disability or a diagnosed illness), there are many additional questions that you need to ask on behalf of your child.

There are five additional areas that a family with a child who has special needs must consider when selecting a childcare facility:

- staff experience working with children with special needs
- support services for children with special needs
- adaptations to the environment, curriculum, and the schedule
- policies that affect children with special needs
- how the center handles medication, chronic illnesses, and allergies

STAFF EXPERIENCE

When you examine the quality of childcare programs, the first characteristic that you need to examine is the staff. Accredited childcare programs may require teachers to obtain an education degree or particular training in the field of early childhood education. Education is extremely important to all teachers, but even teachers who have completed a degree need to have the perspective of being a lifelong learner.

Each teacher needs to make it a priority to continue to learn about the field of early childhood education through professional training and conferences. Education alone will not assist a teacher working with children with special needs. When you decide to leave your child with a teacher, he or she needs previous experience working with the types of disabilities or illnesses that your child has. In a lot of cases, a childcare program may have experience with special needs, but not every teacher may have experience.

It is important for you to ask about the teacher's experience when you tour the program and before your child begins in the classroom. If the teacher has not had *specific* experience with your child's special needs, you should ask if he or she has worked with similar conditions and if the teacher has collaborated with the necessary therapists previously.

If the teaching staff does not have experience working with a condition or illness (like a feeding tube, diabetes pump, or a tracheotomy), it is essential to ask them if they are willing to learn how to assist your child. Most teachers do not learn these skills in school. They learn them when a student in their classroom has the condition and someone trains them on how to take care of the child. On-the-job training is extremely common, but the teacher must be willing and feel comfortable learning how to operate a feeding tube or an insulin pump.

SUPPORT SERVICES

After asking about the classroom teacher who will work with your child, it is also essential to ask about what type of support services that the program can offer to a child with special needs. A childcare program that caters to children with special needs may have therapy staff members (e.g., physical therapists, occupational therapists, speech pathologists, or behavior specialists) on site to work with children who qualify for therapy. This is usually the best scenario, because the therapists have ample opportunities to collaborate with classroom teaching staff.

If you can't find a program with therapists on staff, then it is best to select a program that regularly partners with community therapists that come to the school and work with the children in their natural environment. If the therapists come to the childcare program from an outside organization, then the family will need to sign a release for the therapist to share information with the teachers. If the therapists do not have the time or ability to communicate goals and therapy techniques with the teachers, then it is essential that the family shares the information from the therapists with the teaching staff.

Families also need to think about the student-to-teacher ratios and the classroom sizes when selecting childcare. The childcare program may have ratios and classroom sizes that meet requirements by the state licensing organization or by an accrediting body, but the family needs to see if those ratios and classroom sizes are able to meet the needs of the child's disability.

If there are eighteen preschool children in one classroom, will that volume and level of energy be overwhelming for a child with special needs? If the classroom ratio is one adult for eight students, is that sufficient if your child is unable to feed himself on his own?

Another question to ask a potential childcare program is the percentage of children with typical needs in the classroom compared to the percentage of children with special needs. In order for a child with special needs to function well in the early childhood classroom, he or she must have positive peer role models.

The ratio of children with typical needs compared to children with special needs may vary based on the severity of the needs and the teacher's experience level. If the classroom has children with milder special needs, then it is not as important for the percentage of children with special needs to be as low as if the needs were more significant.

Teacher communication and involvement are essential. If your child has an Individual Education Plan (IEP) and receives therapy from an outside organization, can the center make it possible for the teacher to attend the meetings to offer information about how the child functions in the classroom and if the child is meeting established goals?

The teacher also needs to communicate regularly with the family about how the child is functioning in the classroom. This may require additional parent-teacher conferences or individualized e-mails and phone calls from the teacher. Not every program is willing to spend the extra time to communicate with each family, so make sure that the teachers and administration will put extra effort into the communication process.

ADAPTATIONS TO THE ENVIRONMENT

The physical environment of the childcare program can tell you a great deal about the quality of care that a child may receive at the facility. First, look to see if the facility meets all of the requirements of the Americans with Disabilities Act. Here are a few questions to consider:

- Is the facility wheelchair accessible?
- Is there handicapped-accessible parking to assist families getting their children into and out of the facility?
- Does the classroom look as if a child with a physical impairment could access the whole room?
- Can the teacher see the entire physical environment at one time to see if a child is in need?

Since children with special needs may have physical impairments, there are other aspects of the classroom environment to evaluate. Many children with special needs can be overstimulated by a busy classroom. In order to avoid this type of setting, classroom teachers may alter the room to benefit the children. For example, has the teacher made modifications to the classroom like lowered lighting, soft music playing in the background, or a structured drop-off procedure to keep children calm as they enter the classroom?

Families need to look at both the indoor and the outdoor environment to see if it is appropriate for a child with special needs. The playground needs to have surfacing that allows children with different ability levels to move throughout the playground area. There should be activities on the playground that children can access if they are sitting or standing. It is also helpful if the center regulates a maximum number of children on the playground at one time to reduce the amount of energy and prevent overstimulation.

ADAPTATIONS TO THE CURRICULUM

When you are looking for classroom curriculum appropriate for children with special needs, you need to look for curriculum that is easily adaptable for children of different ability levels. This type of curriculum might allow a more advanced child to begin counting all the red marbles, but it should be adaptable so that another child may be able to sort the marbles by different colors (a pre-math skill).

Since many preschool classrooms are set up to be multiage classrooms (three-year-olds and four-year-olds together in the same room), this is a very common curriculum adaptation. It should also be present in infant and toddler classrooms even though the age span of children in the classroom is typically smaller.

Classrooms should also provide activities that children can do independently and activities that require assistance from a teacher. Typically, most early childhood classrooms have activities led by the teachers during the daily circle time, during small-group activities, or during special art activities.

Because all children are able to focus for different periods of time, there should always be a self-directed activity available for children who cannot sit and focus for an extended activity like circle time or calendar time activities. Independent activities can include dress-up play, puzzles, looking at books, independent art activities, computer play, or sensory activities. These activities are set up to allow children to explore the materials and to learn at their own pace.

Once again, the sensory environment in the classroom is a very important part of the curriculum. Different types of sensory experiences are exceptionally important in a classroom with children who have special needs. Many children with special needs either seek additional sensory experiences or they are defensive to different types of sensory input. Since young children learn a great deal through their senses by touching, tasting, smelling, hearing, and seeing, it is essential to have all of these experiences present in the classroom setting.

All toddler and preschool classrooms should have daily access to a sensory table that is regularly changed to include materials with different textures. Materials in the sensory table can include water, sand, dried corn, shaving cream, Styrofoam peanuts, and other materials that children can easily explore with their hands.

The classroom may also provide items for children to taste if they are seeking extra sensory experiences, like lemon wedges for a sour taste experience or pretzel sticks for a crunchy taste. These oral sensory experiences may prevent some children from seeking sensory experiences in an inappropriate manner.

The classroom staff also needs to be aware that some experiences may be too stimulating for children who are sensory defensive (or those who react violently to sensory experience). This can mean that teachers need to monitor the classroom volume and visual stimulation.

Instead of using a loud voice to yell across the room, the teacher will need to make an effort to walk across the room to speak to a child when necessary. The teacher needs to model this example for the students also. If the teachers would like to play music during the day, they need to consider soft and slow instrumental music instead of loud, fast-paced music with lots of singing that may get the children overly excited.

Sometimes lots of bright, overhead lighting, accompanied with computers being used in the classroom also, can be too stimulating for the children. The use of soft lighting, lamps, or lighting covers can make the classroom much calmer. Teachers also need to consider the types of computer programs that they select for the classroom. It is best to avoid programs with lots of flashing lights or constantly changing screens.

SCHEDULES

The classroom schedule can have as much impact on a child's development and growth as the curriculum. When touring a childcare program, it is very important to ask to see a copy of the classroom schedule. You should be able to see a balance each day between free-play activities and structured activities, between outdoor and indoor activities, and between transitions and extended time on the same activity. Two critical items to examine are the number of transitions and the availability of alternative activities.

Transitions from one activity to another can be challenging for all children, especially for children with special needs. All children need practice on transitioning from one activity to another, but there should not be unnecessary transitions in the school day. Children should have the opportunity to have a stretch of free play during the day when they can make their own transitions, but that free play time should wrap up with a group transition that moves to an activity like circle time or time on the playground.

When the classroom has structured, indoor activities like circle time or a small-group activity, is there an alternative activity if a child cannot or will not participate? For example, if one child cannot sit still for all of the circle time, is it acceptable for that child to leave the circle to participate in another activity once he or she is no longer able to sit still? These are important questions to ask since not all children may be able to attend to an activity for the same amount of time.

Please keep in mind that providing an alternative activity when all the children are in the classroom is very different from providing an alternative activity to playground time. Because childcare programs must keep a required student-to-teacher ratio, it may be impossible to find staffing for one teacher to stay indoors with one child while the rest of the classroom is outside.

POLICIES

One of the first questions that you should ask at every childcare program is to see the policies listed in their handbook for families. Most organized programs have a set list of well-defined policies. Policies for programs designed for children who are typically developing may not meet the needs of a family of a child with special needs. These policies can range from how the center handles late pick-up to when and how to pay tuition, but the policies that are most important for you to be aware of include:

- biting
- toilet training
- transitioning to a new classroom
- classroom placement

Many centers have a biting policy, but each center handles biting very differently. The strictest centers may expel a student from the program after he or she has bitten a certain number of students, but other programs may send a student home for the remainder of the day if he or she has bitten peers that day.

Children with language delays often become biters because they have a hard time getting their point of view across to peers. If you do have a child who bites, you want to find a program that is willing to work with you to eliminate the biting, and possibly collaborate with a therapist if your child is receiving speech therapy, occupational therapy, or Applied Behavior Analysis (ABA) therapy, often used to assist children with autism.

It is also essential to ask the childcare program about their policies on toilet training. Some centers will not allow a child to transition from the toddler program to the preschool program if the child is not completely toilet trained. This can be very challenging for a child with special needs. Most children are toilet trained between two years and four years of age, but every child develops at an individual pace. Typically, young girls may toilet train sooner than young boys, and many little boys are not completely toilet trained until after they turn three years old.

If your child is not toilet trained by the time he or she turns three, how will the preschool program handle it? Will he or she have to stay in a classroom with younger children until toilet training is complete, or will the program make accommodations to the preschool classroom for your child to finish toilet training while in the more advanced classroom? If the child is allowed to move up to the older classroom, does the staff assist the child with diaper changes in the most dignified way, instead of embarrassing that child in front of his or her peers?

Many children struggle with self-care routines but are socially or cognitively ready for a preschool classroom, so these are essential questions to ask before you enroll your child. Also, if a child is struggling with toilet training, it can potentially benefit the child to be in a classroom full of children who model going to the bathroom when they need to do so.

How does the childcare program transition children from one classroom to another? Transitions can be challenging, but moving to a new room, a new team of teachers, and a new group of peers can be an overwhelming experience. The best way to prepare a child for this experience is to plan a transition period where the new teachers initially visit the child in his or her most comfortable environment, and then the child goes to visit the new classroom.

It also benefits the child for the current teachers and the new teachers to communicate with the family about the entire transition process. Children are resilient. They can handle more than is anticipated; however, it is easier on all children to prepare them in the best way possible for the next environment.

Families are always concerned about which classroom and which teacher their children will have once their children begin in a program, but administrators must look at many different factors when they select classroom placements for each child. Most centers look at gender, ability level, personalities that complement one another, and many other factors to place children for a new school year. It is important to know if the school uses a formula for how many children with special needs will be in each classroom.

It is also important to know if children are placed in classrooms strictly by age or strictly by ability level. If a child has turned one year of age but cannot walk, will the school place him or her in the toddler room? Some schools may hold a child back until he or she achieves certain milestones. These milestones may include walking, talking, and being toilet trained.

If your child has a significant special need and will meet these milestones slower than other peers, it is important to discuss how the center will select the best classroom placement for your child. You want your children to be with friends and have appropriate peer models, but you don't want there to be safety concerns. This is a process that must involve the family and the administrators sitting down together to discuss what is best for the child, so make sure that the childcare program you select is willing to do this.

MEDICATION AND ALLERGIES

Many children with special needs may take regular medication or suffer from more significant allergies. This is becoming more common at many childcare programs, so quality early childhood facilities are putting protocols in place to make sure that all children have the ability to stay safe and healthy while in childcare. Here are some of the questions that you should ask if your child takes medication regularly or has extensive allergies:

- Who administers medication? If administrators primarily handle medication distribution, who takes over when the administrator is unavailable?
- Where are medications stored?
- How many staff members are trained on emergency medications like inhalers or EpiPens?
- When a substitute teacher is in the classroom, how do they know which children have extra medical needs?
- If a child has significant food allergies, does the program provide them with an alternative item to eat, or is that the family's responsibility?
- What procedures are in place to eliminate cross-contamination and keep all children safe during the school day?
- What are the school policies on birthday parties or holiday events when families bring food into the school?
- What is the school's policy for medical emergencies? How are the teachers trained for handling a medical emergency?
- Will all the adults working with your child be given the essential information about how to keep your child safe and healthy? When there are teacher changes, how do you update the new staff members?

You may not be able to find a childcare program that has all of these procedures currently in place; however, if you ask the right questions during the enrollment process, you may be able to find a childcare program that is willing to meet the needs of your child once they understand those needs. Starting the communication process during the tour and enrollment is the best way to approach the situation.

- Does the teacher have training in special education?
- Does the teacher have experience working with children who have special needs?
- Does the program offer support services (e.g., occupational therapy, speech pathology) for children with special needs, or is the program willing to collaborate with the private therapist working with your child?
- Are there program policies (e.g., toilet training, classroom placement) that might not accommodate your child's needs?

EIGHT

Infant Childcare

Many families know what to expect when selecting a quality preschool for their young child, but selecting quality childcare for an infant can be much more complicated. First, it can be so challenging to select anywhere to leave your infant. No one is as good as you, so that makes the selection process hard from the beginning.

Once you get to the point where you must select somewhere to care for your child, then the infant room can seem like it is only about basic needs care (e.g., changing diapers, feeding, and sleeping); however, a high-quality infant room has so much more to offer! This chapter will review several factors to consider when you are selecting a childcare program for your young infant:

- Basic care compared to infant curriculum
- American Academy of Pediatrics' Safe Sleep recommendations
- Feeding infants
- Continuity of care compared to rooms by age
- Language-rich environment
- Parent-teacher communication

BASIC CARE COMPARED TO INFANT CURRICULUM

Infants enrolled in a childcare program have several basic needs that must be addressed each day. All infants need to be fed every three to four hours. Young infants will start off with a diet completely based on breast milk or formula, and slightly older infants will begin eating cereal, pureed baby foods, and eventually table food. High-quality infant programs should have some type of private space for a nursing mother to come and feed her child during the day if she has the opportunity, and that space should not comprise solely a closet or a bathroom.

It is also essential that each infant have a diaper change approximately every two hours. This time may vary a slight amount due to the infant's sleep pattern, but during waking hours, the child will need a clean diaper every two hours. Most families in childcare programs use disposable diapers, but if you are considering using cloth diapers, then it is important to know if the center allows cloth diapers.

If the program does allow cloth diapers, then there will probably be regulations on how the soiled diapers must be stored until the family comes to collect them at the end of the day. The family may be required to store them in individual bags and keep all contaminated items in an airtight container. Make sure to ask what each center's policies are if you are considering this option.

Infant classrooms need to allow a child under the age of one to sleep when he or she is tired. Most infants are on a sleep schedule, but due to growth spurts, reflux, illness, or many other reasons, they may have an altered sleep schedule on any given day. This is why childcare providers must follow the infant's needs and allow the child to sleep when he or she appears to be sleepy. Children under the age of one should be sleeping in a crib, and each child should have his or her own crib instead of having to share with a peer.

Each of these basic needs is essential for a quality childcare program; however, the activities in the infant room should only be beginning with basic care needs. Even though it does not look like a preschool classroom, the infant room should have a very structured curriculum.

One of the most important aspects of the infant classroom is having a language-rich environment. Children should have the opportunity to hear words, hear songs, and see words throughout their natural environment. This exposure creates larger vocabularies and earlier readers.

Activities and Lesson Plans

Since so many of the major developmental milestones that occur in the infant room are gross motor skills (large muscle movements), the classroom should be set up to encourage children to move. There should be activity blankets on the floor that encourage infants to spend time lying on their tummies. There should be soft places in the room for children who are first learning to sit so that if they fall, they have some cushion around them. There should be low shelves and tables for young children to pull themselves up to a standing position, and there should be push toys for beginning walkers to use as they learn to take their first steps.

The classroom lesson plans should be posted in a visible location, and they should show that the teachers are reading to the children each day, even if the children are not yet speaking. There should also be a variety of music in the classroom. Recorded music and songs are good tools for the classroom, but you should also see the teachers singing to each child to develop attachment and encourage continued language development.

Lesson plans in the infant room should also include sensory activities and art activities. An infant does not need to be able to sit up at the table in order to participate in art activities. Even young infants who can roll on the floor or lie on their bellies can be a part of a sensory art project. Just learning to place their hands in paint or touch a stamp pad is excellent sensory input for a young child!

These babies can see different colors, feel different textures, and hear the teacher use language to complement the project. Sensory experiences can also include water play activities, hearing different sounds, or using materials like a flashlight in the classroom to show the child different colors and shapes.

The outdoor environment can also be a great tool for teaching infants. Although the teacher needs to be extremely sensitive to extremely hot or cold temperatures, an infant can learn a great deal from the outdoor classroom. Sitting in the grass can allow a child to experience new textures and bright colors. An outdoor stroller ride allows young children to get fresh air and spend time with their teachers and peers. Make sure to ask how and when your child would experience the outdoor classroom as a part of the infant room curriculum.

SAFE SLEEP

High-quality childcare programs must adhere to many different regulations about creating safe sleep environments for young infants. The American Academy of Pediatrics (AAP) endorses very specific recommendations for maintaining safe sleep procedures for children under the age of one.

Not all childcare programs follow all of the AAP recommendations, so it is essential to ask about these recommendations when you first consider enrolling your child in an infant program. Here are different recommendations that the AAP encourages families and childcare programs to follow regarding safe sleep procedures:

- Babies always need to be laid to sleep on their backs in their cribs. Then if the child is able to roll over on his or her own, the child may be left in that position.
- Always dress a baby lightly when lying down to sleep. Do not let an infant get too hot when sleeping.
- An infant should sleep in a crib with a firm mattress and a fitted sheet. There should be no loose bedding in the crib with the child. Loose bedding includes blankets, crib bumpers, stuffed animals, and pillows. Many families desire for their child to sleep with a special stuffed animal during naps and at nighttime; however, when the child is under twelve months of age, there is rarely an emotional attachment to the stuffed animal, and it creates a risk of suffocation.
- A baby may sleep with a pacifier in the crib, as long as it does not have a cord or a clip.
- An infant should only sleep in a basinet or a crib. The baby should never sleep on pillows, bean bag chairs, swings, or high chairs. All of these alternative sleep arrangements can cause safety risks. If the child falls asleep in the swing or bouncy seat, the childcare provider should transfer the child to his or her crib.
- All cribs used in childcare programs must meet safety standards established by the Consumer Product Safety Commission (www.cpsc.gov).
- All children need "tummy time" in order to progress to crawling, but young children who are first learning to play on their tummies need to be closely monitored, especially since they become tired so easily. Never place a young infant in a crib on his or her belly.

Many doctors will suggest swaddling a young infant to help the child calm down and sleep or if the child suffers from acid reflux. Firmly swaddling an infant in a large, thin blanket can prepare the child for sleep by helping the baby to slow down his or her body and feel secure due to the light pressure applied by the blanket. Swaddling can be a controversial process for many childcare programs. When it is done correctly, swaddling can be very beneficial for some infants; however, if a provider does not know how to swaddle correctly, it can have very negative outcomes.

When a childcare provider does not swaddle a baby tightly enough, or with a large enough blanket, then there is often loose bedding in the crib that could cause a suffocation hazard. If the childcare provider swaddles the child too tightly, then it can cause the infant discomfort or even pain.

In order to prevent any liability claims, many early education centers will require the family to sign a release form allowing the childcare provider to swaddle the child while in the infant room. This is another procedure about which each family should ask during the tour and enrollment process.

FEEDING

Every family with an infant has many decisions to make when choosing how they will feed their infant. Initially, you must choose whether the child will have breast milk or formula. The next decision comes when the family must decide when to introduce cereal.

Families have the option to make homemade pureed baby food or to purchase many different types of baby food from a store. This is often when parents decide if they want to introduce typical baby food or implement an all-organic diet.

After pureed baby foods older infants begin to move to soft table foods, and eventually they will begin eating all table foods including proteins. As your infant moves through this process, you want to know that your child's early education program is supporting you and protecting your child's safety.

For a young infant who is primarily drinking out of bottles, the center should have policies on how to heat up the bottles and when the contents of the bottle must be discarded after it has been heated up. After one hour, the bottle should not continue to be offered to the infant, in order to prevent the spread of bacteria.

Childcare providers should always hold an infant while feeding a bottle in order to make sure that the child does not choke while drinking. Also, the center should always use a bottle warmer or a Crock-Pot to warm a bottle. Microwaves can create "hot pockets" inside the bottle that could potentially scald the child, since it may not heat the bottle evenly.

Once the infant begins to transition to cereal and pureed foods, the childcare center needs to make sure that the infant can sit up and maintain good head control in order to prevent choking. Ideally, the child should be double the birth weight. Quality childcare programs will talk with the family about when changes in the diet should occur, and in many programs, the family is required to provide the cereal or pureed food for the child to eat.

As the infant becomes more proficient at eating, the childcare program may be able to provide some soft foods from the school's menu (if the center provides meals). Again, the childcare provider will need to collaborate closely with the family during this time period.

The family may still choose to send table foods from home just to be aware of every ingredient in each food served. The family may also begin to establish a special diet for the child (e.g., all organic foods, vegetarian diet, etc.). As new foods are introduced, the infant may show the initial signs of a food allergy. It is essential for childcare providers to document this information and share it with the parents.

The family should continue to provide breast milk or formula until the child turns one year old. At that point, many childcare centers transition a child to milk. The AAP recommends that children drink whole milk from twelve to twenty-four months of age so that the fat in the milk can assist with brain development and myelinate the passages in the brain. After the child is two years of age, it is recommended to switch to a low fat milk option. It is important to ask the childcare program which option they serve to young children.

When an infant has colic or acid reflux, the doctor may suggest treatment options that do not coincide with the typical AAP feeding recommendations. For example, the doctor may encourage the family to start the infant on cereal sooner than the typical recommendation in order to combat the extra acid in the infant's stomach. Many centers will allow the childcare provider to follow the doctor's recommendation if the family signs a release or if they have the doctor's recommendation in print. Ask the program director how the center handles this type of exception to the rule.

CONTINUITY OF CARE COMPARED TO ROOMS BY AGE

Different early childhood centers move children to the next classroom with different methods. Some centers choose a "Continuity of Care" method, where they keep children in the same classroom for one calendar year (much like a K–12 education model).

In the infant room, this could mean that you have nonmobile and mobile infants grouped in the same classroom. The children have the opportunity to be with the same caregivers for a full year, so there may be a stronger bond between infant and teacher. This can be an excellent benefit during the school year since the teacher knows the children so well, but the stronger attachment can make it more challenging for the infant to transition to a new classroom.

With this style of classroom, as the children age over the course of the school year, the classroom must transform with the children's needs. If the children begin the year as mobile infants just learning to crawl, then they will end the year as young toddlers. This classroom will begin the year with cribs, but they may need to transition the children to nap mats by the end of the year. The toys would have to change over time as well. If the classroom has a broad age span, then there may have to be toys for infants and toddlers both available in the classroom.

Other childcare centers may group their infants and toddlers closer together in age and then move them to the next classroom as they achieve new milestones. For example, a center may have a classroom for nonmobile infants, mobile infants, and young toddlers. The children will spend less time with the teachers in these classrooms, but the teachers will be more specialized to the age group with which they work. Also, there is usually a smaller age span for the children enrolled in each classroom, so the entire classroom should be working on similar skills together.

Each classroom style has specific benefits, but it is important to ask the program director at the time of enrollment which style the center uses so that the family understands how many transitions the child needs to expect and can assist the classroom staff members in making each transition smooth.

LANGUAGE-RICH ENVIRONMENT

One of the biggest indicators of a high-quality infant program is a language-rich environment, but many families do not know what to look for during a tour to see if the environment meets these qualifications. Here is a simple checklist:

- Do the teachers appear to be talking to the infants more than the other adults?
- Are the caregivers making eye contact with the infants when they speak to them?
- Are items in the classroom labeled with printed words?
- Are there age-appropriate books out in the classroom for the children to explore?
- Do the teachers sing to the children?
- Do the teachers read short books to the children?
- Do the adults seem to be taking turns talking with the infants? For example, if the childcare provider says something to an infant, does the provider pause to allow the child to respond with a coo or a repeating syllable sound?
- Is the childcare provider quick to respond if an infant begins to respond? Even if the teacher is tending to the immediate needs of another child and cannot pick up the crying infant, does the provider talk to the child and try to soothe the baby until the teacher is able to physically comfort him or her?
- Do the childcare providers talk to the child during routine care (e.g., changing diapers, feeding, preparing an infant for sleep, etc.) as well as playtime (e.g., playing on the floor, art time, reading a book, etc.)? Many providers will forget that diaper changes and bottle feedings are wonderful opportunities for language development, and a teacher who frequently uses those opportunities has a very language-rich classroom environment!

PARENT-TEACHER COMMUNICATION

The early childhood center that you choose should have classroom and center-wide communication procedures already in place, but when you have an infant in group childcare, there needs to be individual communication methods for every family every day.

Since each infant is so dependent on the caregiver, the family needs to know at the end of each day about the child's eating, sleeping, and diapering behavior throughout the day. This can be done through handwritten notes or through verbal communication with the family. The most successful method is usually a written log with time stamps for each basic care activity that occurred throughout the day.

It is also important for the childcare providers to include individual notes that indicate the infant's temperament and any points of concern (e.g., diaper rash, a reaction after introducing a new baby food, an increased amount of crying during the day). These individual notes will diminish as the child gets older. For example, once a child is in preschool and able to tell the parent about his school day, it is not necessary to document feeding and sleeping habits each day; however, this is especially critical information for a child under the age of twelve months.

Some high-quality early childhood programs may begin offering parent-teacher conferences when a child is enrolled in the infant classroom. Even though the child is extremely young, families need to use these opportunities to communicate with their children's teachers.

These conferences can be used to share information about how to soothe the child, tricks to get the child to sleep, the child's favorite activities at school, or concerns that a child may not be meeting certain developmental milestones. These conferences are an opportunity for both the teacher and the family to learn information about the child. No family should waste these opportunities if they are available.

It can be an emotionally challenging experience for a family to leave a small infant in group childcare for the first time, but there are definitive benefits also. Children learn how to be comforted by more than one person and begin forming healthy attachments with other children and adults. The baby sees other children begin to achieve developmental milestones, like pulling up to a standing position, and then begins to model those behaviors.

Finally, the family feels the support of a fabulous education support team to answer questions and give them feedback to get through challenging situations. Caring for an infant can be very demanding, so it helps every family to have all the support that your community can offer!

- Do the teachers speak to the infants during playtime and during basic care routines (e.g., diapering, feeding, etc.)?

- Does each infant have his or her own crib?
- Does the program follow Safe Sleep practices?
- What type of feeding and sleeping schedule can a child have in the infant classroom?
- How does the program communicate with the families each day about the child's feeding and sleep schedule?
- Does the infant classroom use primary caregivers?

NINE

The Kindergarten Controversy

IS YOUR CHILD READY FOR KINDERGARTEN?

More and more parents are asking themselves, "Is my five-year-old ready to start Kindergarten?" This is a tough question to answer. Kindergarten standards and expectations continue to increase each year.

When Generation X was in Kindergarten, it was a half-day, play-based program that is very similar to today's preschool classroom. Now Kindergarten students typically stay for a full day of school, sit in a desk for most of the day, and are expected to complete challenging academic work.

The main focus of Kindergarten is now reading and writing. Teachers also try to include a great deal of math, science, social studies, computer skills, and fine arts education, but the primary goal for most school systems is to have every child reading by the end of the Kindergarten year.

With the increasing demands of Kindergarten, many parents are asking themselves if their children should start Kindergarten at five years old or if they should defer until the child is six years old. The determining factor for many parents is imagining their children sitting in a desk for the entire school year.

Many early childhood professionals believe that the structure of Kindergarten is not appropriate for a child as young as five years old. However, with the academic demands that are placed on public schools, this is what Kindergarten teachers must do to prepare students for grade-level testing and the next year's content.

More parents are deciding to delay Kindergarten for their children. This means that more families are choosing to wait to start Kindergarten so that the children can grow socially, emotionally, cognitively, and physically.

Families are opting to make this choice especially if their child has a summer birthday or if the child is a boy. Since boys are often very active and less mature than a young girl of the same age, they typically struggle more with sitting still and following directions. An extra year of preschool can allow many students to master some of the social and emotional skills needed to focus, follow directions, and communicate well in the classroom.

If you are considering whether to send your preschooler to Kindergarten next year, there are several factors to consider:

- the age of your child,
- your child's ability to focus for more than a few minutes,
- the cost of an additional year of preschool,
- the activity level of your child,
- your child's school readiness skills,
- the Kindergarten expectations, and
- the recommendation of the preschool teacher.

Some of these factors are very easy to analyze. If a child turns five in November, then he may be able to focus longer and understand the curriculum more than a child with a summer birthday because he has had more opportunity to mature. That may not always be the case, but a few extra months can allow a child's maturity to blossom. Even if your child has a fall or winter birthday, she may not be mature enough for the demands of Kindergarten.

One of the biggest indicators of maturity is how long she can focus on the same activity. This does not include watching television or playing a video game. Can your child complete a task like a puzzle without losing focus? If you try to complete a simple board game or puzzle with your child and you continuously have to bring her attention back to the game, she may not be ready to focus on her assignments yet.

Another factor in the selection process is the cost of preschool. Many families are counting down the days until Kindergarten starts so that they can stop paying large tuition fees for childcare.

If it is not possible for you to pay for another year of preschool, then you always have the option to start your child in Kindergarten and have him or her repeat Kindergarten the following year. At the end of Kindergarten, ask the teacher for a recommendation whether your child is ready for the first grade. If he or she is not ready yet, then you can easily ask the school to hold him or her back in Kindergarten.

Some teachers will encourage you to repeat an additional year of preschool instead of repeating Kindergarten because of the stigma of getting "held back" a year of school. Children in preschool do not typically know when a classmate is repeating a year of school, but some elementary school students have begun to associate repeating a year of school with how smart the child is. This is not as big of a problem in Kindergarten as it is in upper grades, but it is something to consider if you decide to have your child repeat Kindergarten.

Activity Level

How active is your child? Many five-year-old students still need to move in order to learn. They want to explore and use hands-on toys in order to process new information. Most Kindergarten classrooms are not designed for movement.

Even as young as Kindergarten, classrooms can be set up in the same style as a college classroom: the teacher talks from the front of the classroom and the students listen. These classrooms may have a free-choice time during the afternoon when students may choose to do art or read individually, but students primarily learn while sitting in their seats. These same students may only get a brief recess each day and only have physical education once or twice a week.

Not only are children in Kindergarten expected to do work while sitting in their seats, but they also begin the process of academic testing. Of course, these tests are not as demanding as the achievement tests they will see later in elementary school, but a successful kindergartener needs to be able to sit still long enough to complete her assignments and tests. Consider how long your child can sit still when you decide whether she is ready for Kindergarten.

SCHOOL READINESS SKILLS

So many preschool families want to make sure that their children can write their names before they enter Kindergarten. It is important for a child to learn how to write his name, but there are many crucial skills that need to be in place before handwriting. Many

Kindergarten teachers will tell you that it is not essential for a child to come to Kindergarten knowing all of her letters and numbers already. The Kindergarten teacher will review that information with every student.

If a child does not know how to go to the bathroom independently or how to play in a group of friends, then the teachers will have to stop the academic learning in order to make sure that more basic skills are in place. For a child to be completely successful in Kindergarten, he must be prepared in all areas of development (e.g., health and physical development, social and emotional development, self-help skills, language development, gross and fine motor development, and academic skills).

Health and physical well-being must be in place before any higher levels of learning can occur. Children must get enough rest each night in order to come to school prepared to learn, and all children must have enough to eat so that they are not hungry throughout the school day.

If sleep and nutrition are not in place, then the child's body will only focus on those basic needs. Children must come to school healthy in order to perform their best. Children who stay home from school due to illness throughout the school year will not be at school enough to learn essential skills, and children who come to school sick will not be able to focus on their lessons.

This means that all children need to receive their required immunizations and go to the doctor for routine checkups to address health problems as soon as symptoms arise. If a child shows continuous symptoms, like chronic ear infections, then you may need to speak to the doctor about preventative measures to keep him feeling healthy. Also, it is very important for all children starting Kindergarten to have an eye examination to make sure that they can see their books and assignments.

Social and Emotional Skills

A child entering Kindergarten must also have the necessary social and emotional skills. First, a new kindergartener should be able to play with others in a group and share toys with classmates. A Kindergarten student should be able to understand the classroom routine and follow simple classroom rules. Independence skills are important because the student will need to work alone without the constant attention of an adult.

Your child will need to separate from you easily each morning in order to come into the classroom. He or she should be interested in learning new things. It is very important for a kindergartener to focus on a task for ten to fifteen minutes, and he or she should be able to try and fix a problem when something goes wrong. Pre-school teachers typically spend a great deal of time working on these skills because they are so important for Kindergarten success.

Just as it is important for a kindergartener to play independently, it is also important for a Kindergarten student to take care of his or her basic needs independently. Teachers usually refer to these tasks as self-help skills. A Kindergarten student should be completely independent in the restroom, including taking clothing off and putting it on as needed. Although tying shoes may come later in development, he should be able to use Velcro, zip, and snap without any help.

Your child should also be able to eat independently when using a fork and spoon or when eating finger foods. She should be able to cover her mouth when she coughs or wipe her nose when she sneezes. A Kindergarten student should know when he needs to wash his hands and be able to wash them without any assistance.

Another critical skill is keeping track of personal items during the day like a coat, backpack, lunch box, or even a pencil. When a teacher must assist a child who loses his coat or a child who needs help snapping her pants in the bathroom, then the teacher cannot spend time on key academic skills.

Motor Skills

Motor skills include gross motor movements (large muscles) and fine motor skills (using the fingers to manipulate small objects). Children entering Kindergarten must be proficient at both sets of skills. A five-year-old student needs to be able to run, crawl, jump, climb, and skip, but she must also be able to use her gross motor skills to exercise throughout the day as well.

Fine motor skills include the use of crayons, pencils, scissors, zippers, snaps, and buttons. Children with strong fine motor skills can string beads, use tongs, eat with a spoon and fork, unscrew the lid of a jar, and pour water into a cup. Fine motor skills help the children to use their self-help skills, but they are also a key part of handwriting.

Language Skills

Language is one of the most important skills for a kindergartener to have when starting school. Your child must be able to express his wants and needs to others, and he must be able to understand what the teacher and his peers are telling him. Ideally, the teacher would like to see each student arriving for Kindergarten already speaking in five- to six-word sentences. Children should also be able to sing simple songs and repeat short rhymes.

It is especially important that your child can listen to short stories and that she can also tell short stories. She should be able to tell short factual stories, and the teacher wants to know if she can create a story with pretend characters and activities. Language is the largest precursor to reading.

When children can tell a story, they are more likely to listen to a story and then read one. If a child can use many vocabulary words, then he is more likely to learn to write those words and eventually use them in a sentence. Teachers want all of their incoming students to understand and comprehend the use of language, but it is also important that the child can be understood. Expressive language and comprehension are key skills for a successful Kindergarten year.

Academic Skills

Finally, after a long list of characteristics, we can look at your child's academic skills. Teachers would like every child to enter Kindergarten with some basic reading, writing, and math skills. It is important for your child to be able to identify and write her own name. She should also know basic facts about herself like her address, phone number, and birthday.

All children entering Kindergarten should know how a book works, and they should be able to tell the difference between the printed words and the pictures. Each child should know to read a book from the front to the back, and they should know that words start at the left and move to the right.

Your child should be able to recognize environmental print (familiar print) like traffic signs or the McDonald's sign and understand their meanings. He should be able to tell the difference between numbers and letters. The students should be able to identify some uppercase and lowercase letters and numbers.

They should be able to count from one to thirty. Students should be able to sort items based on their differences and their similarities. They should be able to identify colors and shapes, and they should have some basic knowledge about time (day and night, tomorrow and yesterday).

Most children will not enter Kindergarten with all of these skills mastered. Each child has an area or two that still needs some work; however, if you are trying to decide between another year of preschool or moving on to Kindergarten, you should look to see if your child has mastered the majority of these skills.

KINDERGARTEN EXPECTATIONS

You must also consider the expectations of a Kindergarten classroom when you decide if your five-year-old child is ready to begin elementary school. Although the Kindergarten teacher will spend a great deal of time in the first month of school teaching the social expectations of the classroom, the teacher will then expect the children to learn the routine of the day and follow directions so that the entire class can move on to learning curriculum.

Content

It will be essential for Kindergarten students to show independence, the ability to follow multiple-step directions, the ability to sit and focus for extended periods of time, the ability to self-regulate, and the ability to respond to a heavy emphasis on math and reading skills.

Kindergarten students will spend a great deal of time each day sitting at a desk. The amount of time can vary based on whether the classroom is full-day or half-day Kindergarten and how the teacher breaks up the classroom routine. Still, every teacher is expected to teach the children the required core content.

This content includes letter recognition, phonetic recognition (learning the sounds of the letters), beginning handwriting skills, beginning math skills (e.g., one-to-one correspondence, basic addition, graphing, measuring, and money value), science skills (e.g., the seasons, weather, the water cycle, habitats, colors, and plants), and social studies skills (e.g., the community, holidays, safety, and places in the world).

Many schools also include supplementary content on a rotating schedule including visual arts, music, library skills, computers, physical education, and a second language like Spanish. A full-day Kindergarten classroom may spend up to an hour and a half each day just on phonics and handwriting, including small group activities. Half-day classrooms will spend thirty to forty-five minutes each day on phonics and writing.

The students in full-day and half-day Kindergarten classrooms will be sitting at a desk for a large portion of the day, and they will need to focus on the content in order to learn the skills to progress through the school year.

Some five-year-old students are thirsty for this knowledge and drink up everything that the teacher can offer them during the school day, but other students may not be ready to focus on one topic for an extended period of time. You have to know your child and be aware of what she can do in order to decide if she is ready for deskwork.

Routine

Kindergarten will also expect your child to follow multiple-step directions without the teacher giving continuous reminders. Students may be asked to complete a worksheet, take it to the teacher's desk, and then go choose an activity in a classroom center. The teacher will not expect the children to follow all directions at the very beginning of the school year, but after a month or two in the classroom, your child should be able to follow these directions that involve two or three steps.

The teacher will establish a consistent classroom routine so that your child will learn what to expect each day. This will help a young student learn what happens next in the classroom, but the child will still have to complete tasks without the teacher's direct guidance.

Following multiple-step directions is just one skill that your child will require in order to be independent in the classroom. The teacher will expect that each child can take care of his or her basic needs. The child will need to be independent when in the restroom, eating lunch, playing with peers in a group, completing an activity, and cleaning up messes. Every child will need assistance occasionally, but with twenty or more children in most Kindergarten classrooms, the teacher will not be able to assist each child with staying on task.

During morning worktime, the teacher will frequently be leading small-group activities and asking the other children to complete individual assignments. The teacher may not be seated with the children during their lunchtime in an elementary school cafeteria, so it is essential that your child can independently feed himself and clean up after his meal.

There may not be a bathroom inside the classroom, so the teacher may have to send your child down the hallway if she needs to use the restroom during class time. She will need to be able to fasten all clothing and clean herself up by herself. There are some self-help skills that Kindergarten students may still be learning, like tying shoes, but most children should be skilled at taking care of their basic needs.

Self-Regulation

Self-Regulation, the ability to pause between an impulse and an action, is a key skill for Kindergarten. Although teachers do not expect a five-year-old to have this skill mastered, they do expect to see children who are practicing this skill most of the day. For example, a Kindergarten teacher anticipates that some students will cry when they get upset, but the teacher does not anticipate most students to have temper tantrums when they do not get their way during the course of the school day.

By the time a student is five years old, he or she should have enough impulse control to refrain from hitting every child who upsets him or her during the school day. A Kindergarten student should have the impulse control to stay on the playground with the other students when they go outside to play or to stay in line when the class is walking down the hallway.

By the age of five, your child should be able to deal with some frustration or disappointment without large emotional outbursts. Impulse control will help your child to work independently and stay on task during the day with minimal redirection.

Reading and Math Skills

Finally, the Kindergarten classroom expects a large emphasis on reading and math skills. This will be very different for children who have been in a play-based preschool program and have had the freedom to choose the activities they enjoy the most. Of course, all Kindergarten teachers try to make the learning environment fun, but it will not be the same as when your child could spend all morning building in the block area at preschool.

Some students instantly rise to the challenge and love learning new information. They are so proud of their new accomplishments, like learning to read. Less mature Kindergarten students may struggle with their lack of control during the day and the challenge of new academic skills.

If you are trying to choose between Kindergarten and another year of preschool, you should consider how your child will respond to an increase in academics and a decrease in choice through the course of the school day.

THE RECOMMENDATION OF THE PRESCHOOL TEACHER

As a parent, you know your child better than anyone else. You know when your child gets stressed, scared, or angry. You know the things that interest and motivate your child to do better. You love your child and absolutely want the best for him or her.

One thing that you don't get to see that often is how your child behaves during the day at preschool. This is why it is essential to get the recommendation of the preschool teacher before deciding if your child is ready for Kindergarten.

The preschool teacher has the unique opportunity to see how your child functions in a large group of children. Although you can watch closely at home, your child may be playing alone or with one or two siblings. That is always different from being a part of a classroom with fifteen to twenty other children.

In a large classroom, it may be more challenging for your child to work independently, share with others, or come to the teacher when he or she needs help. On the other hand, your child may thrive when he or she is offered the independence and free choice that a large classroom can offer.

Some children perform better in the preschool classroom than parents anticipate because at home there is always an adult offering to assist. When the assistance at school is limited, many children rise to the challenge and complete many tasks independently.

The preschool teacher has been observing your child all year and assessing his or her school readiness skills, so the teacher will be able to offer a strong opinion on whether the child is ready to advance or if he or she would benefit from another year of preschool.

TRANSITIONAL KINDERGARTEN

If you are still confused about sending your child to Kindergarten or repeating another year of preschool, you may want to consider enrolling your child in a Transitional Kindergarten classroom. Transitional Kindergarten is the step in between preschool and Kindergarten.

Transitional Kindergarten implements some of the more structured academic skills of Kindergarten but still uses a more play-based approach to meet the developmental needs of the students. A Transitional Kindergarten classroom does not take the place of Kindergarten, but it is a slightly more challenging alternative than repeating an additional year of preschool.

The Transitional Kindergarten classroom is a more hands-on approach to learning than Kindergarten classrooms, and it still focuses more on self-regulation, self-help skills, and social/emotional skills than Kindergarten. At the same time, there may be short periods when students are seated for group activities or working in small groups with the teacher in order to prepare the children for the rigorous Kindergarten curriculum.

Spending a year in Transitional Kindergarten often helps students master skills that will reduce the chances of retention later in elementary school. The only negative point for many families is that Transitional Kindergarten adds an additional year of schooling for students; however, if you are considering repeating a year of school, then there would be no difference.

Very few public school districts offer a free Transitional Kindergarten program, so the primary providers of Transitional Kindergarten are private schools. The families that often select Transitional Kindergarten for their children typically have children with summer birthdays and would be the youngest students in the upcoming Kindergarten class or the students have fall birthdays and just miss the cut-off for Kindergarten.

The children with summer birthdays often need a little more time to mature and master their social skills before beginning Kindergarten, and the children who have missed the cut-off for Kindergarten are often seeking more challenges than the typical preschool classroom can offer.

Many Transitional Kindergarten classrooms have a higher number of boys enrolled than girls, but both boys and girls can benefit from the content and the hands-on learning approach offered in the classroom.

Finally, many families will enroll their children in Transitional Kindergarten if the children are receiving therapy or early intervention. If your child is struggling with a developmental delay, then a year of Transitional Kindergarten will give him or her an additional year of learning and therapy before starting a more demanding academic schedule.

MAKING THE FINAL DECISION

It is essential to remember that you must make the best decision for your child based on your child's maturity, age, ability to follow directions and focus, and the needs of your family. Many children may have a slow start in Kindergarten but will excel as the school year continues. Ask the recommendation of your child's preschool teacher.

Consider what you know about your child and make the best decision possible. If you support your child and stay involved with his or her education, then it is very likely that he or she will excel in either environment.

- Have you asked your child's preschool teacher if he or she is prepared for Kindergarten or if another year of preschool would be beneficial?
- Do you believe your child is ready to sit at a desk for the majority of the school day and do independent work?
- Is your child able to play well in a group? Can he or she follow multiple-step directions? Is he or she able to take care of personal needs without assistance?
- If your child is not ready for the demands of Kindergarten, do you have access to a Transitional Kindergarten program that incorporates free play with some of the academic demands of Kindergarten?

Appendix 1

Early Childhood Vocabulary

Accreditation

An accredited early childhood program is a program that meets the higher standards of a professional organization like the National Association for the Education of Young Children or the Southern Association of Colleges and Schools. To be accredited by the organization, the early childhood program must go beyond the minimum requirements set by the state licensing organization and demonstrate the best practices of early childhood education.

The accreditation process can take a significant period of time as the school improves its policies, moves through a self-study and creates a portfolio to document its achievements, and then undergoes a site visit by the accrediting organization. Most accreditations last for a limited period of time, like a four-year period, and then the school must go through the reaccreditation process in order to sustain the endorsement of the accrediting organization.

Child Development Associate (CDA) Credential

The CDA is a nationally recognized early childhood education credential offered through the Council for Professional Recognition. CDA candidates must complete 120 hours of formal training and 480 hours of classroom observations before receiving their credential. The training hours are equivalent to approximately two college courses, and candidates can focus their observations toward the preschool classroom or the infant/toddler classroom.

Candidates must also compile a professional portfolio, take an examination on the content of the formal training, and have a CDA specialist complete a formal observation in the classroom while the candidate is working with young children.

Continuity of Care

Instead of moving children to a new classroom each time the child achieves a developmental milestone or at the time of the child's birthday, an early childhood program using a "Continuity of Care" model would attempt to keep the child with the same peer group and the same caregivers for an extended period of time in order to establish attachment and security between the caregivers and the children and between the children and their peers.

Some programs will move children once a year with this model of care, but other programs may use a multiage classroom in order to care for the child in the same environment for an even longer period of time.

Developmentally Appropriate Practice (DAP)

The term *developmentally appropriate practice* means the teacher is selecting activities and planning the classroom environment based on the development level of the children and not simply the age of the students in the classroom. This means that the classroom activities may need to be adapted for children who are developing slightly faster or slightly slower than the developmental norm for the age.

Inclusive

An inclusive early childhood program or classroom allows children with and without special needs to learn and play together in the same classroom environment. Children with special needs are given necessary supports to function to the best of their abilities, and children who are typically developing are also provided with the most developmentally appropriate activities for their ages and ability levels.

Individualized Education Plan (IEP)

An Individualized Education Plan is a plan for a preschool child (or older) who is diagnosed with a developmental delay or a disability. This plan is created by a team composed of a team leader, the child's family or legal guardians, the therapists working with the child to achieve developmental goals, and the child's teacher.

The results of developmental and diagnostic assessment show areas of development with which the child needs additional assistance to achieve, and the team creates a small list of developmental goals based on the assessment data that can be achieved with therapy and classroom supports. In the United States, an IEP is required by the Individuals with Disabilities Education Act if a child has a diagnosed disability or delay.

Individualized Family Service Plan (IFSP)

An Individualized Family Service Plan is similar to an IEP, but it is for children under the age of three years old. Child assessment data is used by a team of professionals to set goals for infants and toddlers who have been diagnosed with a developmental delay or disability. An IFSP is also required by the Individuals with Disabilities Education Act.

Language-Rich Environment

A language-rich environment describes a classroom setting where children hear words and see printed words throughout the environment. This means that the childcare providers actively engage in conversation with the children, and children have conversations with other children throughout the day.

Childcare providers talk to children during play-based activities, but they also take advantage of routine-based activities like diapering, feeding, and sleep routines to talk to children as well. Printed language is displayed throughout the classroom with labels, and children have ample access to writing materials. Books are available to children throughout the day, and teachers may also teach children that pictures and symbols tell a story also (e.g., a stop sign tells cars to stop at an intersection).

Transitional Kindergarten

Transitional Kindergarten is the intermediate step between preschool and Kindergarten. A Transitional Kindergarten classroom would have some of the academic components of Kindergarten like letter recognition, beginning handwriting skills, and learning to count groups of items, but the program will still be more play based than a traditional Kindergarten setting.

With increasing Kindergarten competencies, many families are opting to place their children in a Transitional Kindergarten classroom before beginning Kindergarten. This allows the children more movement during the day with fewer time periods that children are required to sit still and focus on a single activity.

Appendix 2

Resources on Early Childhood Education and Development

American Montessori Society (AMS): www.amshq.org. AMS is a professional development organization for Montessori teachers based on the Montessori philosophy and Nancy Rambusch's interpretation of the Montessori teaching methods.

Association Montessori Internationale (AMI): http://ami-global.org. AMI is a professional development organization for Montessori teachers based on the teaching philosophies of Maria Montessori.

Child Care Aware—A Child Care Resource Organization for Families and Providers: www.childcareaware.org. Child Care Aware is an advocacy organization that helps families find out about what quality childcare is and how to find it.

Council for Professional Recognition: www.cdacouncil.org. The Council for Professional Recognition is the organization that administers the child development associate degree to early education professionals.

HealthyChildren.org: www.healthychildren.org. HealthyChildren.org is a website sponsored by the American Academy of Pediatrics that provides information to families and childcare providers about developmental milestones, reducing illness, preventing injuries, and nutrition.

HighScope: www.highscope.org. The HighScope curriculum and training was created by David Weikart from Ypsilanti, Michigan. This website provides information about this style of early childhood education.

National Association for the Education of Young Children (NAEYC): www.naeyc.org. NAEYC is a professional development organization for childcare providers, and NAEYC supervises a national accreditation program for early childhood education programs.

National Child Care Association (NCCA): www.nccanet.org. NCCA is a professional development and advocacy organization that supports quality early childhood education for all children and policies that support childcare providers and young children.

National Head Start Association: http://nhsa.org. Head Start and Early Head Start are federally funded early childhood programs that focus on early childhood education, health, nutrition, and parent involvement. The National Head Start Association is an organization for educators, families, and community members to advocate for Head Start and receive training about young children.

The Project Approach: projectapproach.org. This website provides information and training about a child-centered curriculum known as the Project Approach.

101

Waldorf Curriculum: www.waldorfcurriculum.com. This website provides information about the Waldorf curriculum created by Austrian educator and philosopher Rudolf Steiner.

Zero to Three: National Center for Infants, Toddlers, and Families: www.zerotothree.org. Zero to Three is an organization that educates childcare providers and families about the development and needs of infants and toddlers. Zero to Three is also an advocacy organization for young children.

Appendix 3

Questions to Ask when Touring a Childcare Program

HEALTH AND SAFETY

- Is there a first aid kit in each room?
- Is there at least one person per classroom with CPR and first aid training?
- Do classrooms maintain low student-to-teacher ratios?
- What is the maximum number of children in each classroom?
- Do both adults and children follow hand-washing procedures in the classroom (e.g., before and after meals, after toileting/ diapering, after coming indoors from the playground, after sneezing, etc.)?
- Are all surfaces used for food cleaned and sanitized?
- Are all surfaces used for diapering cleaned and sanitized?
- Are all medications labeled for the correct child and stored out of the reach of children?
- What is the center's policy on administering medication?
- Are healthy meals served to the children?
- Does the program require immunization records from children enrolled?
- Does the program have an emergency and disaster plan in place that includes natural disasters and relocation if necessary?
- Does the program keep emergency contact information for each child in the individual classrooms?

FACILITY

- Are the building and its furnishings in good repair?
- Do the toys and materials work? Do they have many missing pieces?
- Is there a plan and procedures for facility problems?

STAFF

- Are the staff members nurturing and inviting to the children and the families?
- Does the director have training (a degree) and experience in the field?
- Do the teachers have training (a degree or certification) and experience in the field?
- How long has the teacher been with the center? With that age group?
- Do the teachers/staff receive annual training in the field?
- Do the teachers/staff know how to report if they suspect child abuse?
- Do the teachers have experience working with children with special needs?
- Have the staff all had background checks? Just upon hire or throughout employment?

CURRICULUM

- Do the teachers speak to the infants and toddlers during play-time and during basic care routines (diapering, feeding, etc.)?
- Does each infant have his or her own crib? Does each toddler/preschool child have his or her own mat for nap time?
- Is there a lesson plan available for each classroom?
- Do children have indoor and outdoor play? Group and individual play? Quiet time when needed?
- Are there centers with different types of materials available (e.g., pretend-play materials, blocks, books, art materials, etc.)?
- Do the adults read to the children? Are there words displayed throughout the classroom?
- Are the teachers engaged with students instead of talking to one another?
- Does the curriculum cover more than just art and story time?

ORGANIZATION

- Who runs the program (e.g., director, owner)? Who decides the policies (e.g., owner, board members)?

- Are there established policies or a handbook available to the parents for review?
- Is the program financially sound with no immediate plans to close?
- Does the program accept concerns, grievances, and suggestions from the staff and the families enrolled?
- Does the program meet minimum licensing requirements and post the most current review by the licensing body?
- Does the program hold any type of early childhood accreditation above the minimum state standards for operation?

PARENTS

- Are families welcome in the classroom?
- Are the families given an annual opportunity to evaluate the program?
- Is parent education available through the program?
- Are parent-teacher conferences available?
- Do the families receive a copy of the policy updates/handbook updates annually?

About the Author

Sarah Taylor Vanover has been working in the field of early childhood for over seventeen years. She first began as an assistant teacher in an infant classroom, and since then she has served as a lead teacher, a program administrator, a trainer, and a classroom teaching coach. She is also an adjunct Child Development professor in central Kentucky. Dr. Vanover has also had the opportunity to work at the state level to assist with policy development and supervise early childhood trainers throughout the Commonwealth of Kentucky.

Currently, Dr. Vanover supervises Early Head Start classrooms in the Lexington, Kentucky, area and coaches teachers and program directors on how to improve care in infant and toddler classrooms. Dr. Vanover completed her doctoral work in education policy and leadership and focused her research on what families look for when selecting childcare for their children. She is an active trainer in Kentucky and surrounding states and frequently speaks at conferences on topics like quality childcare indicators, language development in the early childhood classroom, and the importance of assessment in early childhood education.

Dr. Vanover lives in Lexington, Kentucky, with her husband, Rob, and their two sons, Jack and James.